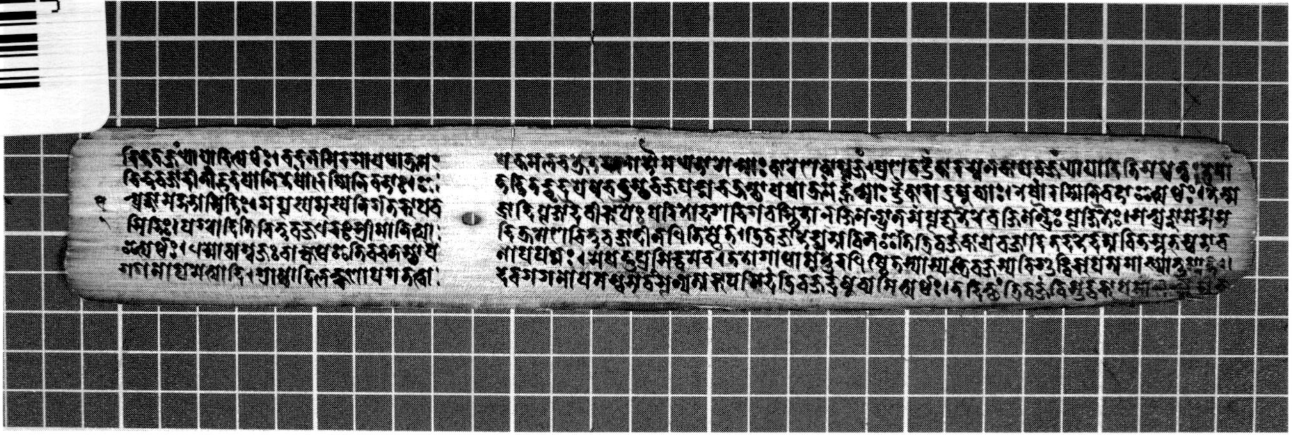

Pra.1697 (kha 2), fol.21b, ©National Archives Nepal

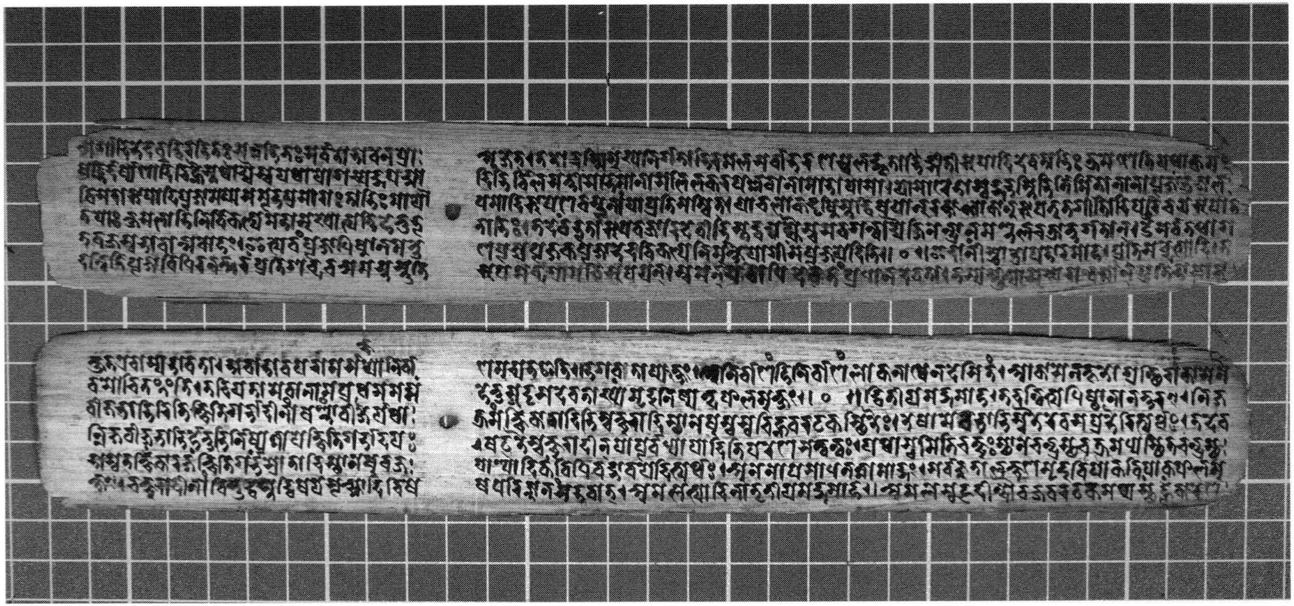

Pra.1697 (kha 2), fol. 28a (top) fol.21a (bottom), ©National Archives Nepal

梵文『普賢成就法註』研究

田中公明

The Sanskrit commentary on the *Samantabhadra nāma sādhana* of Buddhajñānapāda

Introduction, Romanized Sanskrit Text and Translation

Kimiaki TANAKA

渡辺出版 2017

WATANABE PUBLISHING Co., Ltd., Tokyo 2017.

『秘密集会』文殊金剛曼荼羅の諸尊(デルゲ版)

Deities of the Guhyasamāja-Mañjuvajra-maṇḍala (sDe-dge printing press)

目次(Contents)

チベット語要旨(Summary in Tibetan)....5

文献概説....7

Introduction....25

付表(Accompanying Tables and Diagrams)....45

Romanized Sanskrit and English Translation....50

ビブリオグラフィー(Bibliography)....144

あとがき(Postscript)....147

論文の初出一覧....153

著者略歴(About the Author)....154

ブッダジュニャーナパーダ

Buddhajñānapāda

(*Aṣṭasāhasrikā-prajñāpāramitā* pantheon)

༄༅། ། རྒྱ་གར་གྲུབ་ཆེན་སངས་རྒྱས་ཡེ་ཤེས་ཞབས་ཀྱིས་མཛད་པའི་ཀུན་ཏུ་བཟང་པོ་ཞེས་བྱ་བའི་སྒྲུབ་པའི་ཐབས་འདི་ནི། གསང་འདུས་ཡེ་ཤེས་ཞབས་ལུགས་ཀྱི་གལ་གནད་ཆེ་བའི་གཞུང་ཞིག་ཡིན། གཞུང་འདིའི་རྒྱ་དཔེ་བོད་རང་སྐྱོང་ལྗོངས་དུ་བཞུགས་ཡོད་པར་སྣང་ཀྱང་། ངོ་བཤུས་སམ་མ་དཔེ་དངོས་སུ་རྟོགས་ཞིབ་བྱེད་པའི་གོ་སྐབས་མེད། གུས་ཉིད་བལ་ཡུལ་རྒྱལ་ས་ཀ་ཊ་མན་ཌུར་ནང་ཆོས་སློབ་སྦྱོང་དང་ཞིབ་འཇུག་ཆེད་བསྐྱོད་སྐབས་བལ་ཡུལ་གཞུང་གི་དཔེ་མཛོད་ཁང་(National Archives)དུ་ཏཱ་ལ་པ་ཏྲའི་(ཤིང་ལོའི་)ཤོག་བྲིས་པའི་ཀུན་ཏུ་བཟང་པོ་ཞེས་བྱ་བའི་སྒྲུབ་ཐབས་ཀྱི་འགྲེལ་པ་ཞིག་བཞུགས་པའི་ངོ་བཤུས་ལག་སོན་བྱུང་། བལ་ཡུལ་ནས་རྙེད་སོན་བྱུང་བའི་རྒྱ་དཔེ་འདི་བོད་ཀྱི་བསྟན་འགྱུར་ནང་ཀུན་ཏུ་བཟང་པོ་ཞེས་བྱ་བའི་སྒྲུབ་ཐབས་ཀྱི་འགྲེལ་པ་ཁག་བཞི་བཞུགས་ཡོད་པ་དག་ལས་ཐ་དད་པ་ཡིན། དེས་ན་བསྟན་བཅོས་འདིའི་ནང་ལ་དྲངས་པའི་ཀུན་ཏུ་བཟང་པོ་ཞེས་བྱ་བའི་སྒྲུབ་པའི་ཐབས་ཀྱི་ཚིགས་སུ་བཅད་པ་དང་། གསང་འདུས་ཡེ་ཤེས་ཞབས་ལུགས་ཀྱི་གཞུང་གཞན་རྣམས་ལའང་བསྡུན་ནས་རྒྱ་དཔེ་ཞུས་སྒྲིག་གཏན་ལ་ཕབ་པ་ཡིན་ནོ། ། དེར་མ་ཟད་རྒྱ་དཔེ་གཞུང་ཀུན་ཏུ་བཟང་པོ་ཞེས་བྱ་བའི་སྒྲུབ་པའི་ཐབས་ཀྱི་ཚིགས་བཅད་བོད་འགྱུར་བསྟན་འགྱུར་དུ་བཞུགས་ཡོད་པ་དང་། འདིའི་འགྲེལ་པ་ཨིན་སྐད་ཀྱི་བསྒྱུར་པ་དང་མཉམ་དུ་སྐད་གཉིས་ཤན་སྦྱར་བར་སྒྲུན་ཞུས་སོ།། ཞིབ་ཕྲ་ཤེས་པར་འདོད་ན་དཔེ་ཆ་འདིའི་ཨིན་སྐད་ཀྱི་སྔོན་གླེང་(introduction) ལ་གཟིགས་རོགས་གནང་། སྤྱི་ལོ་ ༢༠༡༥ ཟླ་ ༡༡ ཚེས ༢༢ ལ་རྩོམ་པ་པོས་བྲིས།།

文殊金剛

Mañjuvajra

Metropolitan Museum of Art

文献概説

(1)はじめに

『秘密集会』ジュニャーナパーダ流は、パーラ朝初期の密教家でヴィクラマシーラ大寺院の初代金剛阿闍梨となったブッダジュニャーナパーダによって創始された。彼は文殊から『秘密集会』の奥義を伝授され、『大口伝書』*Dvikramatattvabhāvanā nāma mukhāgama*(北京No.2716)・『小口伝書』*Mukhāgama*(北京No.2717)・『普賢成就法』*Samantabhadra nāma sādhana*(北京No.2718、以下*Samantabhadra*と略)などの十四部書を著したといわれる。[1]

これら十四部書の大半は『チベット大蔵経』に収録され、チベット訳を参照することができるが、サンスクリット原典は失われていた。ジュニャーナパーダ流の生起次第の根本典籍*Samantabhadra*のサンスクリット写本も、長らく知られていなかった。なおラーフラ・サーンクリトヤーヤナは、チベットで*Samantabhadra*の註*Sāramañjarī*(北京No.2732)のサンスクリット写本を発見したが、[2]同写本は文化大革命中に行方不明となり、今なお発見されていない。最近、Is.I.A.O.所蔵のトゥッチ・コレクションの中に写真が存在することが判明したが、一般

1 ジュニャーナパーダの略伝と十四部書については、『青史』第7章のye śes źabs lugs kyi skabs (Deb ther sṅon po, Vol.1, 成都 1984, pp.446-452)を参照。

2 Rāhula Sāṅkṛi(sic)tyāyana: "Second Search of Sanskrit Palm-leaf Mss. in Tibet," J.B.O.R.S.,Vol.XXIII, Part I, 1937, p.44に39葉からなるSamantabhadra造のCaturaṅgasādhanaṭīkāの貝葉写本が記載されている。

には公開されていない。[3]

いっぽうラーフラ・サーンクリトヤーヤナがチベットから請来したサンスクリット写本と、チベットで撮影した写本の写真乾板は、パトナのK. P. ジャヤスワル・インスティテュートK. P. Jayaswal Research Instituteが所蔵していたが、ドイツのゲッチンゲン大学が写真を一括購入し、海外の研究者も利用できるようになった。そしてこの中に、ジュニャーナパーダの直弟子ディーパンカラバドラの『吉祥秘密集会曼荼羅儀軌』*Śrī-guhyasamāja-maṇḍala-vidhi-nāma*(北京No.2728)、通称『四百五十頌』が含まれることが分かった。[4]全450偈のうち冒頭から第415偈までが残存しているが、本章(3)で見るように*Samantabhadra*がアーリヤーとギーティの混成調であるのに対し、『四百五十頌』はシュローカで綴られているため、両者の間に同一偈は存在しない。[5]

著者は長らく*Samantabhadra*の原典を探し求めていたが、ネパール留学中に国立公文書館National Archivesに所蔵されるサンスクリット写本

---

3 Sferra: 2008. 45: 30 *Caturaṅgasādhanaṭīkā* (*Sāramañjarī*) of Samantabhadra.

4 Frank Bandurski: "Übersicht über die Göttinger Sammlungen der von Rāhula Sāṅkṛtyāyana in Tibet aufgefundenen buddhistischen Sanskrit-Texte (Funde buddhistischer Sanskrit-Handschriften, Ⅲ)," in Bechert Heinz(ed.), Sanskrit-Wörterbuch der buddhistischen Texte aus den Turfan-Funden, Beiheft 5, Göttingen 1994, pp.113-114に記載されるCod.ms.sanscr.257の5.Mañjuśrīguhyacakra(?)が『四百五十頌』に相当する。

5 2010年にS. S. Bahulkarが、サールナートのCIHTSから校訂テキストを刊行した。

pra.1697(kha 2)[6]のマイクロフィルム[7]を入手し、帰国後にその内容を検討したところ、著者不明の*Samantabhadra*の註の断片であることを発見した。これは従来、「何かの仏教タントラの註釈」*Kasyacid bauddha-tantrasya ṭīkā*[8]と称され、内容が明らかでなかった写本である。(以下サンスクリット註と略)

写本のサイズは縦4.5cm×横30.5cmで、*Bṛhatsūcīpatram*には７葉と記載されるが、実際には８葉ある。各葉の裏面左側には、フォリオ番号がネワール数字で記入されている。[9]それによれば、残存する８葉は第21葉から第28葉までであることが分かる。なお末尾の第28葉の裏面は、剥落により文字の判読が困難で、第29葉以後が失われてから、かなりの年月が経過したことを示唆している。文字はブジモールBhujimol体[10]で、１葉に５〜６行が書写されている。

なお『チベット大蔵経』には*Samantabhadra*の註が４篇収録されるが、本写本は、これらの何れとも完全には一致しない。しかしdPal kun tu

6 なおpra.はprathamaの略で、その最終番号1697番は雑多のSkt.写本の集成である。この中には後述のŚiṣyānugrahaなど、他にも貴重な文献が含まれている。

7 NGMPP,Reel No.A994/8、なおNGMPPでは、Bauddhatantraという仮題が付されている。

8 Bṛhatsūcīpatram, Bauddhaviṣayaka Vol.1, Kathmandu Vikrama saṃvat 2023 (≒1967 A.D.), p.97.

9 ネワール数字によるフォリオ番号の記述については、田中公明・吉崎一美『ネパール仏教』(春秋社、1998年) pp.95-97を参照。

10 ネワール文字の書体については、Hemaraj Sakya, Vikrama saṃvat 2030 (≒1974 A.D.) を参照。

bzaṅ po造とされる*Sāramañjarī*(以下SMと略)[11]とは近接した関係にあり、全く同文と思われる箇所も少なくない。

このサンスクリット註は、*Samantabhadra*の全文を逐語的に釈しているわけではない。したがって釈文からジュニャーナパーダの原文を完全に復元することはできないが、従来、チベット訳のみで原語が分からなかったジュニャーナパーダ流の術語の多くが回収できたことには、大きな意味がある。

また*Samantabhadra*と『四百五十頌』の比較により、ジュニャーナパーダが用いた用語の多くが、ジュニャーナパーダ流の相承者に影響を及ぼしたことも分かった。このように本写本は、わずか貝葉8葉の断片ながら、ジュニャーナパーダ流の生起次第の根幹部分を扱っており、貴重な写本といえる。

なお著者が田中 2010の第2部に本写本の邦訳を発表後[12]、加納和雄が、ラサのチベット博物館に展示されていた樺皮の古写本が*Samantabhadra*の梵本であることを発見した。[13]しかし彼は、連続する2葉の片面のローマ字化テキストを発表するにとどまった。加納のテキストは、*Samantabhadra*の第19偈から第54偈に相当するが、これはサンスクリット註が残存している部分の直前に相当する。

(2)全篇の構成

11 Caturaṅga-sādhana-ṭīkā-sāramañjarī-nāma(北京No.2732)。SMにパラレルな釈文が存在する部分は、第3章のローマナイズと訳で適宜参照した。

12 田中公明『インドにおける曼荼羅の成立と発展』(春秋社、2010年)pp. 507-550.

13 加納和雄「普賢成就法の新出梵文資料について」『密教学研究』第46号(2014年)

つぎに*Samantabhadra*の全体的な構成と、サンスクリット註が残存している部分の概要を見ることにしたい。(45頁の表参照)

*Samantabhadra*には、2種のチベット訳がある。本節では、主としてリンチェンサンポ訳によって、その構成を見ることにしよう。まず全体は、165偈からなる。[14]

松長有慶が明らかにしたように、*Samantabhadra*には『秘密集会タントラ』との共通偈や真言が多数含まれている。しかしそれ以外の部分に関しては、リンチェンサンポ訳が9音節4句によって1偈をなすのに対し、スムリティ訳は13ないし19音節2句によって1偈を構成している。[15]またその内容にも若干の異同があるため、両者が同一のテキストから訳出されたかは疑問とされていた。なお*Samantabhadra*の韻律については、次節で詳しく論じることにする。

後期密教の生起次第は、①初加行三摩地ādiyoga nāma samādhi②最勝曼荼羅王三摩地maṇḍalarājāgrī nāma samādhi③最勝羯磨王三摩地karmarājāgrī nāma samādhiの三種三摩地よりなる。そして*Samantabhadra*では、①初加行三摩地が第3偈から第69偈、②最勝曼荼羅王三摩地は第70偈から第108偈、③最勝羯磨王三摩地は第109から末尾の165偈までに相当する。

そしてサンスクリット註は、①初加行三摩地の途中の第54偈から、②最勝曼荼羅王三摩地の末尾近くの第105偈までを註している。

このうち①初加行三摩地は、行者が瑜伽観法によって本尊と合一するという、成就法の中心をなす重要な次第である。そしてこの部分に

14　*Samantabhadra*の偈番号は、金本拓士によっている。

15　松長有慶『密教経典成立史論』(法藏館、1980年)pp.255-256.

は、ジュニャーナパーダ流の生起次第の根幹をなす「四支」caturaṅgaの解説が見られる。いっぽう最勝曼荼羅王三摩地は長大なので、ジュニャーナパーダ流を特徴づける文殊金剛十九尊曼荼羅の生起(第70偈から第93偈)と、生起した曼荼羅の諸尊への灌頂と供養(第94偈から写本末尾)の２節に分割して、ローマ字化テキストと英訳を収録した。

(3) *Samantabhadra*の韻律とレトリック

著者が明らかにしたように、ネパール撰述の密教儀軌*Mañjuvajra-mukhyākhyāna*には*Samantabhadra*の第10偈から第18偈までが「懺悔」pāpadeśanāとして引用されている。[16]いっぽう契丹の慈賢訳『妙吉祥平等祕密最上觀門大教王經』(大正No.1192)には、「黙念大伽陀」として同一部分が第19偈まで２度に亙って漢字で音写され、最初の引用箇所には意訳も付されている。[17]

その後の調査で、この偈はケンブリッジ大学所蔵の密教儀軌Add.1708(Ⅲ)や*Śiṣyānugraha*[18]の冒頭など、ネパールで発見された多くの密教儀軌にも、出典を明らかにすることなく引用されていることが判明した。

このうち慈賢の漢字音写は、原則として１偈を４句に訳出している。ところが復元された第10偈から19偈までは１pādaの音節数が一定せず、韻文であるのか明確でなかった。ところがサンスクリット註の第95偈

16　拙著『インド・チベット曼荼羅の研究』(法藏館、1996年)の第10章「『普賢成就法』と『秘密集会』ジュニャーナパーダ流曼荼羅」

17 大正No.1192, Vol.20, 905c-906c.

18 National Archives Nepal, pra.1697 (kha 2).

の釈に、「《蓮華の中》で始まり、供養で終わる６首のアーリヤーによって、その儀軌を仰せられた。」[19]とあることから、『秘密集会』からの引用偈を除く*Samantabhadra*の全文が、アーリヤー調で綴られている可能性が出てきた。

そこで第10偈から第18偈が、この韻律に合致するかを調査した。アーリヤーは、１pādaの音節数を限定せず母音の長短のみによって律せられる。そこで各pādaの母音数を、韻律上短い母音を１、長い母音を２として計算したところ、アーリヤー（12-18-12-15）・ギーティ（12-18-12-18）の２種の韻律が検出された。

アーリヤーやギーティの場合、第１と第２、第３と第４pādaを接合し、１偈を２行で書く場合が多い。スムリティの１偈を２行とする訳出方法は、このようなアーリヤー調の綴り方を模倣したものと考えられる。

残念ながらサンスクリット註は、*Samantabhadra*の偈全体を引用していない。したがって註釈から本偈を復元することは困難であるが、リンチェンサンポとスムリティが、ジュニャーナパーダによる他の偈も同様の体裁で訳出していることから、『秘密集会』からの引用を除く*Samantabhadra*の全文が、アーリヤーとギーティで綴られていた可能性が高くなった。[20]

つぎにサンスクリット註から抽出された*Samantabhadra*の本文を用いて、リンチェンサンポ・スムリティ両訳の相違を検討してみよう。

第56偈にĀḥ daṅ Oṃ niとある部分は、スムリティ訳ではA daṅ phyag

---

19 tam vidhi[ṃ] kamalodara ityādinā āryāṣaṭkena pūjāparyantenāha/

20 加納の研究も、著者の推定を裏づけている。（加納 2014, 69）

’tshal gñis kyisとなって意味不明だったが、回収されたサンスクリットではOṃ字がpraṇavaと表現されており、スムリティはこれをpraṇamaと誤認してphyag ’tshal[21]としたらしい。

いっぽう第55偈のsvahṛdīndauは、スムリティ訳ではraṅ sñiṅ zla ba'iと正しく訳されているが、リンチェンサンポ訳では、字数の関係でraṅ zla yisと省略されている。このように註から回収された原文によって、両者の訳文の相違を合理的に説明できることが少なくない。したがって両者は、ほぼ同文のサンスクリット韻文を、別の体裁で訳出したものと判明した。

*Mañjuvajramukhyākhyāna*等から回収された原文からは、ジュニャーナパーダが晦渋な偈文を好んだことが看守できる。また一偈中に同系統の音(歯音や歯擦音)を多用したり、同音反復(sasutasugata; satsattva)の常用も顕著である。なお3種のネパール系サンスクリット写本は、このような難解な箇所においてしばしば混乱を示しており、書写した者も正しく意味を把握していなかったことを示している。

いっぽうサンスクリット註からは、四忿怒の一尊ヤマーンタカを説く第86偈では、YamāntakaがVaivasvantāntakārin(ヴィヴァスヴァト神の子＝ヤマを調伏するもの)[22]と表現され、「蛇によって身体の四肢を装飾せり」は、krūrabhujaṅgāṅgai[r] bhūṣaṇaḥと綴られていることが判明した。これもantāntaとかaṅgāṅgaという、同一音の反復を故意に用いた

21 デルゲ・チョネ両版ではphyag mtshanとなっているが、ナルタン・北京両版のphyag 'tshalの方が正しい。

22 正しくはVaivasvatāntakārinとすべきだが、写本ではVaivasvantāntakārinと綴られている。

ものと思われる。

*Samantabhadra*の原文は一部しか回収されていないので、全貌は明らかにできないが、ジュニャーナパーダが用いた修辞法は、正統的なalaṅkāraのように技巧的ではなかったと思われる。しかしアーリヤーという大衆的な韻律の採用とも相まって、このような通俗的なレトリックが他所にも用いられていた可能性は十分に考えられる。

(4) 四支瑜伽

*Samantabhadra*は別名Caturaṅgasādhanaとも呼ばれるように、「四支瑜伽」の体系を特徴としている。そしてサンスクリット註の①初加行三摩地の部分には、「四支」についてのまとまった解説が見られる。その写本上の位置は、残存部分の頭に当たる第21葉の1行目(21a1)から、第23葉の裏1行目(23b1)までに相当する。

すでに松長博士が指摘したように、「四支」caturaṅgaとは親近sevā・近成就upasādhana・成就sādhana・大成就mahāsādhanaの四種を指す[23]が、サンスクリット註は、これに上・中・下の三品を立て、都合十二支を分立している。またサンスクリット註は、下品のsevāの途中より、中品のmahāsādhanaまでを①初加行三摩地とする。これに対し上品の四支は、②最勝曼荼羅王三摩地に配される(表1参照)。

23 松長有慶『密教経典成立史論』(法藏館、1980年)p.158他

表１　三品の四支

下品mṛdu	第65偈	最上uttama	初加行三摩地
中品madhya	第66～69偈		
上品adhimātra	第70偈～	通sāmānya	最勝曼荼羅王三摩地

このうち下品の四支は、行者が、本尊を生起し(sevā)、感覚器官を加持し(upasādhana)、身口意の三業を加持し(sādhana)、灌頂を受けることで(mahāsādhana)、自己を浄化して本尊と一体化する次第であり、先行する瑜伽タントラの初加行三摩地を継承するものである。これに対して中品の四支は、行者のパートナーとなる女性(明妃)を観想し、これを自身と同様のプロセスで浄化する次第で、後期密教独自のものといえる。

古典的なインド思想では、絶対者Brahmanは中性原理であったが、後にはシヴァ・ヴィシュヌ等の男性神格が主宰神の地位を占めるようになる。仏教のsādhanaでも、瑜伽密教までは男性のiṣṭadevatāが好まれたが、後期密教では絶対者をyuganaddhaつまり男女性の合一と考えるので、男性がsādhakaとなる場合は、女性のパートナーを必要とする。サンスクリット註では、このような男女性をVajradhara=prajñāと称し、チベット仏教では、これを因の持金剛と呼ぶ。彼らを因hetu・出生者janakaとして曼荼羅を出生するのが、後期密教の生起次第の特徴といえる。

ジュニャーナパーダ流のcaturaṅgaに関しては、吉水千鶴子が1985年に東京大学に提出した修士論文(未刊)で取り上げている。吉水によれば、ヴィタパーダの*Samantabhadra*の釈[24]に四支を三品に分ける説が見られるとのことだが、サンスクリット註とヴィタパーダ註の間には若干の差違が認められる。また四支を等流・異熟・士用・離垢の四果に配する方軌(表2)もヴィタパーダと一致している。このうち離垢果は、『阿毘達磨倶舎論』の離繋果visaṃyogaphalaに相当すると考えられるが、本写本では原語がvaimalyaphalaとなっており、一致しない。

つぎに四支がどのような理由で、アビダルマの五果説と結びついたのか、考えてみよう。まずsevāと等流果については、釈に記述があるように、因たる尊devatā—この場合は文殊金剛—に相似な尊が、果として生じるからと考えられる。

表2　四支瑜伽

四支瑜伽	四果
親近sevā	等流niṣyanda果
近成就upasādhana	異熟vipāka果
成就sādhana	士用puruṣakāra果
大成就mahāsādhana	離垢vaimalya果

また四支の最終段階たるmahāsādhanaにおいては、灌頂を受けて本尊との合一が完成するので、これが解脱を意味する離垢果に配されたことも理解できる。ところが異熟果と士用果については、なぜこのよう

24 Caturaṅga-sādhanopāyikā-samantabhadrā-nāma-ṭīkā(北京No.2735)

に配当されるのか、明確な説明がなされていない。

いっぽうサンスクリット註の第65偈の釈では、下品mṛduの四支が最上uttamaとも形容されるが、これは矛盾ではない。すでに吉水が指摘したように、「四支」には、上述の三品への分類法の他に、最上uttamaと通sāmānyaに分類する説があり、それに従ったものと思われる。ちなみに本文献では、最勝曼荼羅王三摩地所説の上品の四支が、「通の四支」とされている。最勝曼荼羅王三摩地は、ジュニャーナパーダ流を特徴づける文殊金剛十九尊曼荼羅の出生を主な内容とするが、そのプロセス自体は、主尊だけでなく曼荼羅の全尊格に共通するので、「通」sāmānyaと称されたのである。

そこでサンスクリット註所説の四支の関係を整理すると、表1と2のようになる。

(5) 文殊金剛十九尊曼荼羅

つぎに②最勝曼荼羅王三摩地の部分は、ジュニャーナパーダ流の文殊金剛十九尊曼荼羅の諸尊の出生を扱い、内容のほとんどは図像学的言及で占められている。写本上の位置は、第23葉の裏面1行目(23b1)から、第27葉の表3行目(27a3)までに相当する。なお諸尊の配置については、本書48頁の図を参照されたい。

それではサンスクリット註所説のジュニャーナパーダ流『秘密集会』曼荼羅について概観してみよう。*Samantabhadra*では、第72偈から78偈までに五仏、第79偈から83偈に四仏母、第84偈に六金剛女、第85偈から91偈に四忿怒が説かれている。なお六金剛女の記述が他に比して簡略なのは、これらが『秘密集会』「第一分」所説の根本十三尊に含まれず、ジュニャーナパーダによって付加された尊格群であることを暗示している。

またこの曼荼羅については、佐藤努が、主として*Samantabhadra*のチベット訳に基づいた研究を発表している。[25]サンスクリット註に説かれる十九尊曼荼羅も、これと本質的に異なるところはないので、今回は写本を解読して新たに判明した事実と、著者の解釈が佐藤と異なる点のみを指摘するにとどめたい。

佐藤の指摘のうち最も重要な点は、主尊が文殊金剛であるか阿閦であるかという問題である。これについてサンスクリット註は、その第73偈の註において、つぎのように述べている。

vajradhṛg ity utsargamantreṇa saṃcodya **saṃhṛtavye**(legs bsdus) ti {/} vipañcita[s]pharaṇādyākārasaṃhāreṇānīya **sarvabhāvena** (dṅos po thams cad kyis ni) sarvātmanā ātmani Mañjuśrīrūpe **nive**[24a4]**śayet** (źugs par bya)/

「vajradhṛkという出生真言によって驚覚して、《収斂させるべし》とは、広大に拡散した姿を収束させつつ導いて、《全霊をもって》つまり全力を尽くして、自身すなわち文殊師利の姿の中に《導き入れるべし》」

このようにサンスクリット註では、十九尊曼荼羅の主尊を、vajradhṛkを心真言とする阿閦を文殊の中に遍入させた尊格、つまり文殊金剛と解釈している。これは、佐藤が指摘したラトナーカラシャー

25 佐藤努「ジニャーナパーダ流のマンダラ構成」(『密教図像』第14号、1995年)

ンティなどの阿閦＝文殊金剛同躰説に近い解釈といえよう。[26]

またスムリティ訳において宝生が宝主Rin chen dbaṅ phyug、白衣が最勝母となっている点であるが、第75偈のサンスクリット註を見ると、

Ratneśa[ṃ][24b2]Ratnasaṃbhavaṃ ratnadhṛg iti saṃcodya Mañjuvajrasya dakṣiṇato dhyāyād iti sambandhaḥ/

「ratnadhṛkという出生真言によって《宝主》Ratneśaつまり宝生Ratnasambhavaを驚覚して、文殊金剛の《南に》観想すべしというようにつながる。」とある。

なお佐藤がスムリティ訳Rin chen dbaṅ phyugから予想した原語は*Ratneśvaraだが、サンスクリット註から原語がRatneśaであることが分かった。ちなみにRatneśaは、ジュニャーナパーダ流と関係が深い『時輪タントラ』などで、Ratnasambhavaの別名として再三出現する語である。したがって宝主は宝生と同躰であり、単に韻律上の都合でRatneśaと綴られた可能性が強い。

これに対して白衣(パーンダラー)が「最勝母」yum mchogとなる点は、白衣を説く第81偈の前半部が逐語的に註されていないため明確でないが、著者は「最勝母」は白衣の別名ではなく、「最高の仏母」を意味する一般名詞であると考えている。

(6)諸尊の灌頂と供養

26　メトロポリタン美術館所蔵の文殊金剛像(本書6頁参照)では、上部の阿閦の図像が*Samantabhadra*第72～73偈のSkt.註に一致するのに対し、文殊金剛の左右の第2手は弓箭を持ち、阿閦と図像が微妙に異なるのは示唆的である。

このように*Samantabhadra*では、文殊金剛十九尊曼荼羅を生起した後、第95偈以下で、曼荼羅の生起で出生した諸尊を灌頂し供養する次第が説かれる。その写本上の位置は、第27葉の表面3行目(27a3)から、第28葉の末尾までである。なお本写本では、最終フォリオ裏面(28b)の保存状態が悪く、文字が一部しか判読できない。

いっぽうその内容は、①第95～100偈と供養加持真言pūjādhiṣṭhāna-mantra[27]、②第101～105偈までに分かれる。

このうち第95偈の釈に、「《蓮華の中》(＝第95偈の初句)で始まり、供養(の真言)で終わる6首のアーリヤーによって・・・(諸尊の)輪を供養すべき方軌が説かれた。」とあるように、①第95～100偈は、最勝曼荼羅王三摩地の前半部で出生した文殊金剛十九尊曼荼羅の諸尊を供養する方軌を説いている。

これは実際の供養物を使用するのではなく、観想によって供養物を奉献する運心供養の一種といえる。しかしそこには、後期密教を特徴づける性的な観想が導入されている。その方軌は、自らの身体に導き入れられた諸尊が、菩提心(精液)となって妃の蓮華(女性器)に放出され、そこから六つの感覚対象を象徴する六金剛女が生まれ、諸仏を供養すると観想するのである。なおこの供養には、最勝曼荼羅王三摩地の冒頭、上品の四支の第一支において文殊金剛十九尊の出生に用いられた観想法が応用されている。

なお田中 2010の「研究篇」第5章[7]では、『秘密集会』の金剛女と呼ばれる女性尊が、金剛界曼荼羅の八供養菩薩から発展したことを論じたが、ここでは六金剛女が、まさに供養菩薩としての役割を果たし

---

27 松長有慶『秘密集会タントラ　校訂梵本』(東方出版、1978年)p.17.

ているのを見ることができる。

いっぽう第101偈以降は、「讃の奉献」stotropahāraと規定されるように、『秘密集会』曼荼羅の根幹をなす五仏の讃を説く。まず一切の声境(聴覚の対象)を、木霊のように(実体がないと)考え、自らの心に本尊、すなわち曼荼羅の主尊を観想し、諸法を讃頌の音となす。(第101偈)

なお、ここで引用される五仏の讃(第102～106偈)は、『秘密集会』「第十七分」第１～５偈に相当するが、松長校訂テキストと比較すると、一部の語句に出入が見られる。[28]そしてサンスクリット註は、第105偈の阿弥陀如来讃(『秘密集会』第十七分第４偈)の冒頭で終わっている。

(7)ローマ字化テキストと和訳

著者はネパールから帰国後、本写本のローマ字化テキストを複数の学術誌に発表してきた。これらの論文は、15年ほどの間に逐次執筆されたため、テキストの整定方針や訳の書式に不一致が認められた。そこで著者は、これらを一部改訂して和訳を付し、著者の博士論文である田中2010「文献篇」(2007)の第３章として収録した。

次章では、写本が残存している部分のサンスクリット註を、[1]初加行三摩地・[2]最勝曼荼羅王三摩地から文殊金剛十九尊曼荼羅の生起・[3]生起した諸尊の灌頂と供養の３節に分割し、*Samantabhadra*の本偈と対照させたローマ字化テキストを左頁に、右頁には左頁に対応する

28 なお本書所収テキストでは、Skt.註と一致する異読を採用している。

サンスクリット註の英訳を掲載することにした。[29]なおサンスクリット註の日本語訳は、すでに田中2010で発表したので、本書には掲載しなかった。

なお*Samantabhadra*の完全なサンスクリット・テキストは、いまだ公刊されていない。いっぽう加納のテキストは、サンスクリット註が残存している部分の直前で終わっている。しかし第59偈から第63偈、第102偈から第105偈までは『秘密集会タントラ』からの引用なので、タントラから回収したサンスクリット原文を掲載した。それ以外の本偈については、リンチェンサンポ訳・スムリティ訳の順でチベット訳を掲げた。なお本偈のチベット訳は、中国蔵学研究中心編『丹珠爾』所収本[30]を底本とし、ナルタン(N.)・デルゲ(D.)・北京(P.)・チョネ(C.)の各版から、サンスクリット註から回収された原文に一致する訳を採用した。チベット語のローマ字転写は、米国国会図書館Library of Congress式によっている。

また対照に便利なように、本偈からの引用はボールド体で表示し、それに対応するチベット訳を(　)に入れて示した。

本写本はネパール系写本の常としてbaとvaの区別がなく、saとśaもしばしば混同されている。適宜訂正したので、詳細はローマ字化テキス

29　本写本は天下の孤本で、完全に一致するチベット訳も存在しないので、著者の能力では完全な校訂テキストを整定することができない。本書では、一応読解可能なローマ字化テキストの提出を目標とした。

30　中国蔵学中心編『丹珠爾』(対勘本)第21巻(中国蔵学出版社、1998年)pp.905-926; pp.927-946. なお『丹珠爾』では、スムリティ訳の第81偈から122偈までが欠落しているので、デルゲ版・北京版に基づいて補足した。

トに付した註を見られたい。

なお[...]は汚損・剥落による判読不能を表し、[ ]は脱字と思われる箇所を修補した部分、これに対して{ }は、写本に存在する文字や記号が不要であることを示し、{_ _}とした箇所は、文字や記号が抹消記号parimārjitasaṅketaにより筆誅されていることを示す。また写本では、sattvaが常套的にsatvaとなり、レーパ直後の子音が重複するなど、現在とは異なった正書法が見られるが、次章ではそのまま転写している。

Introduction

(1) Previous Studies

The Jñānapāda school of the *Guhyasamāja-tantra* was established by Buddhajñānapāda, a renowned esoteric Buddhist who lived during the early Pāla dynasty. He was appointed the first vajrācārya of Vikramaśīla monastery. It is also recorded that Buddhajñānapāda was initiated into the mysteries of the *Guhyasamāja-tantra* by Manjuśrī and wrote fourteen works, including the *Dvikramatattvabhāvanā nāma mukhāgama* (P. 2716), *Mukhāgama* (P. 2717), and *Samantabhadra nāma sādhana* (P. 2718; hereafter: *Samantabhadra*).[1]

We can refer to most of these fourteen works since they are included in the Tibetan Tripiṭaka, but their Sanskrit originals have been lost. The Sanskrit manuscript of the *Samantabhadra*, the basic text on the *utpattikrama* of the Jñānapāda school, had for a long time remained undiscovered. During his expedition to Tibet, Rāhula Sāṅkṛtyāyana discovered the Sanskrit manuscript of the *Sāramañjarī* (P. 2732), a commentary on the *Samantabhadra*.[2] However, this manuscript went missing during the Cultural Revolution and has not yet been found. Recently, photographs of this manuscript were identified in Tucci's

1 For a brief biography of Jñānapāda and his fourteen major works, see "Ye śes źabs lugs kyi skabs" in the *Blue Annals* (*Deb ther sṅon po*, vol. 1, Chengdu, 1984, 446–452).

2 There is mention of a palm leaf manuscript of the *Caturaṅgasādhanaṭīkā* by Samantabhadra, consisting of 39 folios, in Saṅkṛtyāyana 1937, 44.

collection in the Is.I.A.O. Library,[3] but they have not yet been made publicly available.

The Sanskrit manuscripts and photographs of them which Rāhula Sāṅkṛtyāyana brought back from Tibet had been kept at the K. P. Jayaswal Research Institute in Patna. But recently Göttingen University purchased them, and it has become possible for overseas researchers to refer to them. The *Śrī-guhyasamāja-maṇḍala-vidhi-nāma* (P. 2728), commonly known as the "450 verses," by Dīpaṅkarabhadra, a direct disciple of Buddhajñānapāda, turned out to be included among them.[4] I purchased the CD-ROM from Göttingen University and began to study this manuscript. It is considered valuable since it contains 415 verses out of the 450 verses in total. However, as is discussed in section 3 below, in contrast to the *Samantabhadra*, the metre of which is a mixture of āryā and gīti, the "450 verses" are ślokas, and the two texts do not share any identical verses.[5]

I had long been searching for a Sanskrit manuscript of the *Samantabhadra*, the basic text on the *utpattikrama* of the Jñānapāda school, and while studying abroad, I eventually came across a manuscript entitled *Kasyacid*

3 Sferra: 2008. 45: 30 *Caturaṅgasādhanaṭīkā* (*Sāramañjarī*) of Samantabhadra.

4 Sanskrit manuscript Cod. ms. sanscr. 257, 5. Mañjuśrīguhyacakra(?) listed in Bandurski 1994, 113–114, corresponds to the "450 verses."

5 In 2010, S. S. Bahulkar published the text as *Śrīguhyasamājamaṇḍalavidhiḥ* (Sarnath: CIHTS).

bauddhatantrasya ṭīkā[6] (pra. 1697 [kha 2])[7] at the National Archives in Kathmandu. I procured a microfilm copy,[8] and upon examining it after my return to Japan, I was able to ascertain that it is an incomplete commentary on the *Samantabhadra* by an unknown author (hereafter referred to as the Sanskrit commentary).

The size of the manuscript is 4.5 cm in height and 30.5 cm in width and consists of eight folios, although the *Bṛhatsūcīpatram* describes it as consisting of seven folios. The folio numbers are written in Newari numerals in the left margin of each folio.[9] Judging from these folio numbers, the extant eight folios correspond to folio nos. 21–28. The verso of the last folio (28b) is difficult to read because of damage. This would suggest that the folios from no. 29 onwards were lost a long time ago. The script is Bhujimol,[10] and each folio contains five or six lines.

Four commentaries on the *Samantabhadra* are preserved in the Tibetan

---

6 *Bṛhatsūcīpatram*, Bauddhaviṣayaka vol. 1, Kathmandu, Vikrama saṃvat 2023 (≒ 1967 A.D.), 97.

7 Pra. is an abbreviation of prathama and its final number 1697 consists of miscellaneous Sanskrit manuscripts. These include important manuscripts such as the *Śiṣyānugraha* described below.

8 It corresponds to NGMPP, Reel No. A994/8. The NGMPP has assigned the provisional title Bauddhatantra.

9 On folio numbers using Newari numerals, see Tanaka & Yoshizaki 1998, 95–97.

10 On the various Newari scripts used in Sanskrit manuscripts, see Hemaraj Sakya, Vikrama saṃvat 2030 (≒ 1974 A.D.).

Tripiṭaka, but none of these is in complete accord with the manuscript in question. This manuscript is, however, closely allied to the *Sāramañjarī*[11] (hereafter: SM) attributed to dPal kun tu bzaṅ po, and there are numerous passages that seem to be identical.

This Sanskrit commentary does not provide a word-for-word commentary on the *Samantabhadra*, and so we cannot completely restore the full text of Jñānapāda's original work. However, it is significant that the hitherto unknown original Sanskrit forms of Jñānapāda's terminology, known only from the Tibetan translation, can be restored.

A comparison of the *Samantabhadra* with the "450 verses" has made it clear that much of Jñānapāda's terminology influenced later successors of the Jñānapāda school. Thus, this manuscript, in spite of the fact that only eight folios have survived, is important because it explains the main part of the *utpattikrama* of the Jñānapāda school.

After the publication of the Japanese edition of this book, corresponding to Part II of my dissertation,[12] Kanō Kazuo 加納和雄 identified a Sanskrit manuscript of the *Samantabhadra* among the exhibits at the Tibet Museum in Lhasa. However, he transcribed only a single side of two consecutive folios that happened to be exhibited at the time. Kanō's edition corresponds to vv. 19–54 of the *Samantabhadra*, which immediately precede the extant Sanskrit

11 *Caturaṅga-sādhana-ṭīkā-sāramañjarī-nāma* (P. 2732). I refer in the romanized text to the *Sāramañjarī* when parallel passages are found in it.

12 Tanaka 2010.

commentary.[13]

(2) Overall Structure of the *Samantabhadra*

Next, I wish to survey the overall structure of the *Samantabhadra* and give an outline of that part for which the Sanskrit commentary survives (see table on p. 46). Two Tibetan translations of the *Samantabhadra* are included in the Tibetan Tripiṭaka, and I shall survey the structure of the *Samantabhadra* by referring mainly to Rin chen bzaṅ po's translation.

First, the *Samantabhadra* consists of 165 verses.[14] As Matsunaga had made clear, the *Samantabhadra* incorporates many verses and mantras from the *Guhyasamāja*. However, except for the verses incorporated from the *Guhyasamāja*, in Rin chen bzaṅ po's translation each verse consists of four lines of nine syllables each, while in Smṛti's translation each verse consists of two lines of thirteen to nineteen syllables each.[15] There are also some minor differences with regard to content, and there had been some doubt as to whether they were in fact translations of the same text. The metre of the *Samantabhadra* will be discussed in the next section.

The *utpattikrama* of late tantric Buddhism consists of three *samādhi*s: 1. *ādiyoga nāma samādhi*, 2. *maṇḍalarājāgrī nāma samādhi*, and 3. *karmarājāgrī*

---

13 Kanō 2014.

14 The verse numbers of the *Samantabhadra* follow the numbering of Kanamoto Takuji 金本拓士.

15 Matsunaga 1980, 255–256.

nāma samadhi. In the *Samantabhadra*, the *ādiyoga nāma samādhi* corresponds to vv. 3–69, the *maṇḍalarājāgrī nāma samādhi* to vv. 70–108, and the *karmarājāgrī nāma samadhi* to vv. 109–165, the final verse. The surviving part of the Sanskrit commentary covers the verses from v. 54, belonging to the *ādiyoga nāma samādhi*, to v. 105, near the end of the *maṇḍalarājāgrī nāma samādhi*.

Among these three samādhis, the *ādiyoga nāma samādhi* is an important procedure constituting the core of the *sādhana*, in which the practitioner unites himself with the principal deity. In the commentary on this part there is found an explanation of the "four limbs" (caturaṅga), the core of the *utpattikrama* of the Jñānapāda school. The commentary on the *maṇḍalarājāgrī nāma samādhi*, on the other hand, is quite detailed. Therefore, I have divided it into two parts—the genesis of the 19-deity maṇḍala of Mañjuvajra (vv. 70–93) and the consecration of the generated maṇḍala deities and offerings to them (v. 94 to the end of the manuscript)—and an English translation has been attached to the romanized text.

(3) The Metre and Rhetoric of the *Samantabhadra*

I have already pointed out elsewhere that vv. 10–18 of the *Samantabhadra* are quoted in a Sanskrit manuscript of Nepalese origin entitled *Mañjuvajra-mukhyākhyāna* as verses of repentance (*pāpadeśanā*).[16] Likewise vv. 10–19

16 Chapter 10, "The *Samantabhadra nāma sādhana* and the Guhyasamāja-maṇḍala of the Jñānapāda School" in Tanaka 1996.

appear twice in transliterated form as a "great *gāthā* to be recited silently" in the *Miaojixiang pingdeng bimi zuishang guanmen dajiaowang jing* 妙吉祥平等秘密最上觀門大教王經 (Taishō no. 1192), translated into Chinese by Cixian 慈賢 of Qidan 契丹 during the Northern Song 北宋, and in the first instance they are accompanied by a Chinese translation.[17]

Subsequent investigations have revealed that these verses are also quoted without any indication of their source in numerous Buddhist tantric manuals discovered in Nepal, including Cambridge University's Add. 1708 (III) and the *Śiṣyānugraha*[18] (National Archives of Nepal, pra. 1697 [kha 2]).

Cixian translated each verse into 4 *pāda*s. Meanwhile, in the restored Sanskrit verses 10–19 the number of syllables in each *pāda* is not fixed, and it was not clear whether or not they had in fact been composed in metrical verse. In the Sanskrit commentary on v. 95, however, it is stated that "he gave directions by means of six *āryās* starting from 'inside the lotus' and ending with offerings,"[19] and this would suggest that the entire text of the *Samantabhadra* apart from quotations from the *Guhyasamaja-tantra* may have been composed in the *āryā* metre.

The *āryā* is a form of metre in which the number of syllables in each *pāda* is not fixed, and instead it is governed by vowel length alone. An examination of the restored verses revealed that they evidence two kinds of metre, *viz.* the *āryā*, consisting of 12, 18, 12 and 15 *mātrā* or morae, and the *gīti*, consisting of 12, 18,

17 Taishō no. 1192, vol. 20, 905c–906c.

18 National Archives of Nepal, pra. 1697 (kha 2).

19 *tam vidhi[ṃ] kamalodara ityādinā āryaṣaṭkena pūjāparyantenāha/*

12 and 18 *mātrā*.

In the case of the *āryā* and *gīti* metres, the first and second *pādas* and the third and fourth *pādas* are often combined and each verse is written as only two lines. It is possible that Smṛti's method of translation, with each verse consisting of two lines, is modelled on this way of writing verse in the *āryā* metre.

Unfortunately, the Sanskrit commentary does not cite entire verses of the *Samantabhadra*. Therefore, it is difficult to restore the original verses on the basis of the Sanskrit commentary. However, there is a high probability that all verses of the *Samantabhadra* except for quotations from the *Guhyasamāja* were composed in the *āryā* and *gīti* metres since Rin chen bzaṅ po and Smṛti translated other verses in the same format.[20]

Next, I wish to compare the two Tibetan translations on the basis of the Sanskrit text of the *Samantabhadra* retrieved from the Sanskrit commentary. First, the phrase in v. 56 that was translated by Rin chen bzaṅ po as *Aḥ daṅ Oṃ* has been translated by Smṛti as *A daṅ Phyag 'tshal gñis kyis*, the meaning of which had been unclear. In the Sanskrit text, however, *Oṃ* is expressed as *praṇava*, and so it would appear that Smṛti mistook this for *praṇama*, which he rendered by *phyag 'tshal*.[21]

The phrase *svahṛdīndau* appearing in v. 55, on the other hand, has been correctly translated by Smṛti as *raṅ sñiṅ zla ba'i*, while Rin chen bzaṅ po has abbreviated it to *raṅ zla yis* for metrical reasons. There are many similar

20 Kanō's study also supports my assumption (Kanō 2014, 69).

21 D. C. have phyag mtshan, but N. P. phyag 'tshal is correct.

instances in which it is possible to explain in rational terms differences in the two Tibetan translations on the basis of the Sanskrit text retrieved from the Sanskrit commentary. It is thus evident that both Tibetan versions were translated from more or less identical Sanskrit verse texts but in different styles.

It is to be observed from the Sanskrit verses restored from the *Mañjuvajra-mukhyākhyāna* and other texts that Buddhajñānapāda had a predilection for obscure diction. He also makes repeated use of similar sounds (e.g., dentals and sibilants) within the same verse and is wont to repeat identical syllables (e.g., *sasutasugata*, *satsattva*). It may be noted that the three Nepalese manuscripts show evidence of considerable confusion in difficult passages such as these, thus indicating that the scribes themselves did not have a correct grasp of the meaning.

The Sanskrit commentary also shows that in v. 86, dealing with Yamāntaka, one of the four gatekeepers, Yamāntaka is referred to as *Vaivasvantāntakārin* ("he who destroys the son of Vivasvat [= Yama]")[22] and *krūrabhujaṅgāṅgai[r] bhūṣaṇaḥ* ("he whose limbs are adorned with fierce snakes"). These locutions too were presumably chosen on account of the repetition of identical sounds in *-antānta-* and *-aṅgāṅga-*.

The Sanskrit text of the *Samantabhadra* has been retrieved only in part, and so full details remain unclear, but it would seem that Buddhajñānapāda's rhetoric was not as elaborate as that of orthodox *alaṅkāra*. There is, however, a strong possibility that, in conjunction with his adoption of the *āryā* metre with its popular appeal, he used elsewhere too commonplace rhetorical techniques

22 Gramatically, it should be *Vaivasvatāntakārin*.

such as those noted above.

(4) The Four Limbs

As is indicated by the fact that it is also called *Caturaṅgasādhana,* the *Samantabhadra* is characterized by the system of "four limbs" (caturaṅga). The Sanskrit commentary contains an explanation of the four limbs in its commentary on the *ādiyoga nāma samādhi*, corresponding to the section from the start of the extant folios (21a1) to 23b1.

Table 1. Four Limbs in Three Grades

lower (mṛdu)	–v. 65	supreme (uttama)	*ādiyoga nāma samādhi*
middle (madhya)	vv. 66–69		
upper (adhimātra)	v. 70–	common (sāmānya)	*maṇḍalarājāgrī nāma samādhi*

It has already been pointed out by Matsunaga Yūkei 松長有慶 that the four limbs refer to *sevā*, *upasādhana*, *sādhana*, and *mahāsādhana*.[23] However, the Sanskrit commentary of the *Samantabhadra* subdivides each of these into upper (*adhimātra*), middle (*madhya*), and lower (*mṛdu*) grades, resulting in a total

23 Matsunaga 1980, 158, etc.

of twelve limbs. The Sanskrit commentary starts from midway through v. 54, which corresponds to the final section on *sevā* of the lower grade, and the eight limbs consisting of the lower and middle grades of the four limbs all come under the *ādiyoga nāma samādhi*, while the four limbs of the upper grade are allocated to the *maṇḍalarājāgrī nāma samādhi* (see Table 1).

The four limbs of the lower grade constitute a process whereby the practitioner purifies himself and becomes one with his chosen deity by generating the deity (*sevā*), empowering his sense organs (*upasādhana*), empowering his body, speech, and mind (*sādhana*), and being consecrated (*mahāsādhana*), and they may be said to represent a development of the *ādiyoga nāma samādhi* of the antecedent Yoga tantras. By way of contrast, the four limbs of the middle grade constitute a process for visualizing the practitioner's female partner and purifying her in the same manner as he has purified himself, and they are distinctive of late tantric Buddhism.

In classical Indian philosophy, Brahman, the absolute, was neuter. However, in later Hinduism male deities such as Śiva and Viṣṇu came to occupy the position of supreme god. In Buddhist *sādhana*s up to the Yoga tantras, a male tutelary deity (iṣṭadevatā) was favored. But in late tantric Buddhism the absolute was regarded as *yuganaddha,* the union of the male and female deities. Therefore, in the case of a male practitioner, he needs a female partner. The Sanskrit commentary refers to such a couple as "Vajradhara = prajñā," and Tibetan Buddhism calls such a generator "causal Vajradhara" (rgyu'i rdo rje 'chaṅ). Making them the cause (hetu) or generator (janaka) for generating the maṇḍala is a characteristic of the *utpattikrama* of late tantric Buddhism.

The four limbs in the Jñānapāda school have been discussed in detail by

Yoshimizu Chizuko 吉水千鶴子 in her master's thesis submitted to the University of Tokyo in 1985 (unpublished), and according to her research a subdivision of the four limbs into three grades can also be found in Vitapāda's commentary on the *Samantabhadra*,[24] although there are some differences in their content. The four limbs are also associated with four results referred to as "cognate result" (*niṣyanda-phala*), "matured result" (*vipāka-phala*), "co-operative result" (*puruṣakāra-phala*), and "untainted result" (*vaimalya-phala*), and these too are mentioned by Vitapāda (see Table 2). The "untainted result" presumably corresponds to the "disjunct result" (*visaṃyoga-phala*) of the *Abhidharmakośa-bhāṣya*, but the term appearing in the Sanskrit commentary is *vaimalya-phala*, not *visaṃyoga-phala*.

Let us now consider why the four limbs were linked to the Abhidharma theory of five results. First, *sevā* may be assumed to have been associated with the "cognate result" because, as is explained in the Sanskrit commentary, a deity similar to the deity, Mañjuvajra in this case, constituting the cause arises as a result.

Likewise, the final limb of *mahāsādhana* may be understood to have been associated with the "untainted result," corresponding to liberation, because the practitioner is now consecrated and achieves union with his chosen deity. However, as regards the "matured result" and "cooperative result," no clear explanation is given for their association with *upasādhana* and *sādhana* respectively.

---

24 *Caturaṅga-sādhanopāyikā-samantabhadra-nāma-ṭīkā* (P. 2735)

Table 2. Four Limbs and Four Results

four limbs	four results
sevā	niṣyanda-phala
upasādhana	vipāka-phala
sādhana	puruṣakāra-phala
mahāsādhana	vaimalya-phala

Meanwhile, in the commentary on v. 65 the four limbs of the lower grade are also described as "supreme" (*uttama*), but this does not involve any contradiction, for, as has already been pointed out by Yoshimizu, in addition to the aforementioned subdivision of the four limbs into three grades, they are also subdivided into "supreme" and "common" (*sāmānya*), and the above comment is probably an allusion to this. In the Sanskrit commentary the four limbs of the upper grade, corresponding to the *maṇḍalarājāgrī nāma samādhi*, are referred to as the four "common" limbs. The *maṇḍalarājāgrī nāma samādhi* consists primarily of the generation of the 19-deity maṇḍala of Mañjuvajra, which is distinctive of the Jñānapāda school, but it was regarded as "common" because this process of the generation is applied to all the deities of the maṇḍala, rather than only to the principal deity as was the case in the *Ādiyoga*.

The various associations involving the four limbs in the Sanskrit commentary are set out in Tables 1 and 2.

(5) The 19-deity Maṇḍala of Mañjuvajra

Next, the *maṇḍalarājāgrī nāma samādhi* explains the generation of the 19-deity maṇḍala of Mañjuvajra, which is distinctive of the Jñānapāda school. Most of it consists of iconographical descriptions, and it corresponds to folios 23b1–27a3 in the manuscript. Regarding the arrangement of the deities, reference should be made to the table on p. 49.

Let us now survey the Guhyasamāja-maṇḍala of the Jñānapāda school on the basis of the Sanskrit commentary. In the *Samantabhadra,* the five Buddhas are explained in vv. 72–78, the four Buddha-mothers in vv. 79–83, the six adamantine goddesses in v. 84, and the four wrathful deities in vv. 85–91. The description of the six adamantine goddesses is simpler than that of the other deities. This suggests that they were not included in the thirteen basic deities explained in Chapter I of the *Guhyasamāja* and were added by Jñānapāda himself.

Satō Tsutomu 佐藤努 has already written about this maṇḍala, mainly with reference to the Tibetan translation of the *Samantabhadra.*[25] Since the 19-deity maṇḍala explained in the Sanskrit commentary is essentially the same, I will only note some new findings gained through the study of the Sanskrit commentary and some differences of interpretation between Satō and myself.

The most important issue raised by Satō is that the main deity of the maṇḍala is Akṣobhya or Mañjuvajra. In this regard, the Sanskrit commentary, in its comments on v. 73, reads as follows:

25 Satō 1995.

> vajradhṛg ity utsargamantreṇa saṃcodya **saṃhṛtye** (legs bsdus) ti {/} vipañcita [s] pharaṇādyākārasaṃhāreṇānīya **sarvabhāvena** (dṅos po thams cad kyis ni) sarvātmanā atmani Mañjuśrīrūpe **nive** [24a4] **śayet** (źugs par bya) /
>
> One should arouse [Akṣobhya] with "Vajradhṛk," the mantra of emission. "Having contracted," [that is to say,] having gathered and drawn in the manifold rays that have emanated, the [yogin] should merge them completely into himself as Mañjuśrī.

Thus, the Sanskrit commentary interprets the main deity of the 19-deity maṇḍala as Mañjuvajra, namely, Akṣobhya, whose seed-syllable is *vajradhṛk* and merges into Mañjuśrī. This interpretation may be similar to that of Ratnākaraśānti and others noted by Satō.[26]

Regarding the point that Smṛti translated Ratnasambhava as *rin chen dbaṅ phyug* and Pāṇḍarā as *yum mchog* ("supreme mother"), the Sanskrit commentary, in its comments on v. 75, explains this as follows:

> Ratneśa[ṃ] [24b2] Ratnasaṃbhavaṃ ratnadhṛg iti saṃcodya Mañjuvajrasya dakṣiṇato dhyāyād iti sambandhaḥ/

---

26 In an image of Mañjuvajra held by the Metropolitan Museum of Art (cf. p. 6), the iconography of the effigy of Akṣobhya on the top of the halo coincides with that of Cittavajra (= Akṣobhya) as explained in the Sanskrit commentary on vv. 72–73. The second hands of the principal image, Mañjuvajra, on the other hand, hold a bow and an arrow respectively. This fact is suggestive.

> The sentence is completed as follows [by supplying the subordinate and main verbs]: arousing [him] with [the mantra] "Ratnadhṛk," one should contemplate Ratnasambhava (<Ratneśa) to the south of Mañjuvajra.

Satō restored the original Sanskrit of Smṛti's translation *Rin chen dbaṅ phyug* as *Ratneśvara. However, the Sanskrit commentary indicates that it is Ratneśa. This Ratneśa frequently occurs as an epithet of Ratnasambhava in the *Kālacakra-tantra*, which has close connections with the Jñānapāda school, and other tantric scriptures. Therefore, Ratneśa and Ratnasambhava are identical, and Ratneśa may have been used simply for metrical reasons.

As for the point that the *Samantabhadra* makes Pāṇḍarā the "supreme mother" (*yum mchog*), this is not clear since the Sanskrit commentary does not give a word-for-word commentary on the first half of v. 81. However, my view is that "supreme mother" is not an epithet of Pāṇḍarā but a common noun.

(6) Consecration of Deities and Offerings

Starting from v. 94, the *Samantabhadra* describes the consecration of the maṇḍala deities that have been generated in the foregoing sections and the procedures for offerings and songs of praise. This corresponds to the section from folio 27a3 to the end of folio 28. However, the recto of folio 28 is severely defaced and almost illegible.

The contents of this section can be divided into two sections: vv. 95–100 and the mantra for the empowerment of offerings (*pūjādhiṣṭhānamantra*),[27] and vv. 101–105.

In the comments on v. 95, it says: "[Now] in the six *āryā* [verses] that begin with the word 'in the lotus' and end with [the explanation] of the offerings, he explains the procedure by which one is to worship the assembly of deities after it has been consecrated in this way." Thus, vv. 95–100 explain the method whereby one makes offerings to the nineteen deities of the Mañjuvajra-maṇḍala generated in the former part of *maṇḍalarājāgrī nāma samādhi*.

It is not an actual offering but an ideal offering which the practitioner visualizes in the offering process. However, it includes sexual visualization. Namely, the practitioner draws the maṇḍala deities into his body, and they transform into *bodhicitta* (= semen) and are ejaculated into the vagina of the consort. The six adamantine goddesses, who symbolize the six sense fields, are born from this, and they make offerings to the Buddhas. In this offering, the visualization of the genesis of the nineteen deities of the Mañjuvajra-maṇḍala at the start of the *maṇḍalarājāgrī nāma samādhi*, corresponding to the first limb of the upper four limbs, is applied.

As I argued in Chapter 5 of Tanaka 2010, the adamantine goddesses of the *Guhyasamāja* evolved from the eight offering goddesses of the Vajradhātu-maṇḍala. Here, the six adamantine goddesses do indeed play the same role as offering goddesses.

From v. 101 onwards, the songs of praise for the five Buddhas, the principal

27 Matsunaga 1978, 17.

members of the Guhyasamāja-maṇḍala, are explained, as is indicated by the fact that these verses are named "offering of praise" (*stotrohāra*). First, all sounds are considered to have no substance, just like an echo. Next, contemplating the main deity in one's heart, one transforms all *dharma*s into the sounds of a eulogy (v. 101).

Here, the *Samantabhadra* cites the songs of praise for the five Buddhas (vv. 102–108) from *Guhyasamāja* XVII (vv. 1–5). However, if we compare them with Matsunaga's edition of the *Guhyasamāja*, several inconsistencies in wording can be detected.[28] Further, the Sanskrit commentary ends at the beginning of the song of praise for Amitābha (v. 105), namely, v. 4 of *Guhyasamāja* XVII.

(7) Romanized Text and English Translation

After my return from a period of study in Nepal, I published on several occasions the romanized text of different sections of the Sanskrit commentary on the *Samantabhadra*. However, these articles contained some inconsistencies since they appeared in different academic journals over a period of more than fifteen years. Therefore, I revised them and included the entire text of the Sanskrit commentary together with the Japanese translation in my dissertation entitled *Genesis and Development of the Maṇḍala in India*, submitted to the University of Tokyo in 2007.

28 In the romanized text, I have adopted the variant readings that coincide with the Sanskrit commentary.

In the following chapter I have divided the extant text of the Sanskrit commentary[29] into three parts: 1. *ādiyoga nāma samādhi*, 2. the generation of the 19-deity maṇḍala of Mañjuvajra from the *maṇḍalarājāgrī nāma samādhi*, and 3. consecration of generated maṇḍala deities and offerings to them. I have presented on the left-hand side of the page the romanized text of the Sanskrit commentary and on the right-hand side the English translation of the commentary. I have not included the Japanese translation of the Sanskrit commentary since it has already been published in Part II of Tanaka 2010.

The complete Sanskrit manuscript of the *Samantabhadra* has not yet been discovered. Kanō's aforementioned romanized edition (vv. 19–54) does not cover the part for which the Sanskrit commentary is extant. However, vv. 59–63 and vv. 102–105 are quoted from the *Guhyasamāja-tantra*. Therefore, I have presented the original Sanskrit verses restored from the *Guhyasamāja*. As for the other verses, I have given the Tibetan translations by Rin chen bzaṅ po and Smṛti. The transcription of the Tibetan translation is based on China Tibetology Research Center 1997[30], and I have adopted the variant readings from the sNar thang (N.), sDe dge (D.), Peking (P.) and Cone (C.) editions that coincide

29 This manuscript is a unique manuscript, and there is no Tibetan translation that coincides completely with it. Therefore, it is very difficult to prepare a perfect diplomatic edition. In this book, I have accordingly attempted to provide a romanized text capable of being read with some degree of comprehension.

30 China Tibetology Research Centre, *bsTan 'gyur*, vol. 21, 1998, 905–926, 927–945. However, vv.81-122 of Smṛti's translation are lacking in the CTRC edition. I supplemented them on the basis of the sDe dge and Peking editions.

with the original Sanskrit restored from the Sanskrit commentary. The transcription of Tibetan characters follows the Library of Congress (U.S.A.) system.

To facilitate the reader's understanding of the relationship between the original verses and the Sanskrit commentary, I have shown words quoted from the original verses in bold typeface and given the corresponding Tibetan translation in parentheses. When translating the Sanskrit commentary, I have employed the special symbol "<". For example, "(*sarvabhāvena<sarvātmanā*)" appearing in the English translation means that *sarvabhāvena* occurring in the original verse has been paraphrased as *sarvātmanā* by the author of the Sanskrit commentary.

As is common in Nepalese manuscripts, the manuscript does not distinguish between *ba* and *va*, and there is also frequent confusion of *sa* and *śa*. These have been corrected. For details, reference should be made to the footnotes added to the romanized text.

When missing glyphs or glyphs that are illegible on account of soiling of the palm leaves have been augmented on the basis of quotations from or parallel passages in other texts, these have been enclosed in square brackets ([ ]). Redundant glyphs and symbols in the manuscript have been enclosed in braces ({?}), while redundant glyphs that have been deleted in the manuscript with the deletion sign (*parimārjita-saṅketa*) have been enclosed in braces and underlined.

In addition, *sattva* and *tattva* are regularly written *satva* and *tatva*, while a consonant after *r* (*repha*) is doubled, but these and other discrepancies with standard orthographical practice have been transcribed as they are.

『普賢成就法』*Samantabhadra nāma sādhana* の構成

<table>
<tr><th>三種三摩地</th><th>写本</th><th>論　文</th><th>四支</th><th>偈番号</th><th>内　容</th></tr>
<tr><td rowspan="2"></td><td rowspan="3">欠</td><td rowspan="3"></td><td rowspan="2"></td><td>第１～９偈</td><td>序と前行</td></tr>
<tr><td>第10～17偈</td><td>懺悔</td></tr>
<tr><td rowspan="3">初加行
三摩地</td><td rowspan="2">下品</td><td>第18～54偈</td><td rowspan="2">自己の浄化</td></tr>
<tr><td rowspan="5">残
存</td><td rowspan="2">『＜我＞の思想』
前田専学博士
還暦記念論集</td><td>第55～65偈</td></tr>
<tr><td>中品</td><td>第66～69偈</td><td>妃の浄化</td></tr>
<tr><td rowspan="5">最勝
曼荼羅王
三摩地</td><td>『密教図像』16</td><td>上品</td><td>第70～94偈</td><td>曼荼羅の出生</td></tr>
<tr><td rowspan="2">『東洋文化
研究所紀要』
150冊</td><td rowspan="5"></td><td>第95～100偈</td><td>供養</td></tr>
<tr><td>第101～105偈</td><td rowspan="2">讃</td></tr>
<tr><td rowspan="3">欠</td><td rowspan="3"></td><td>第106偈</td></tr>
<tr><td>第107～108偈</td><td>五甘露の奉献</td></tr>
<tr><td>最勝羯磨王
三摩地</td><td>第109～165偈</td><td></td></tr>
</table>

Synopsis of the *Samantabhadra nāma sādhana*

<table>
<tr><th>Three Samādhis</th><th>Manuscript</th><th>References</th><th>Four Limbs</th><th>Verses</th><th>Contents</th></tr>
<tr><td rowspan="2"></td><td rowspan="3">missing</td><td rowspan="3"></td><td rowspan="2"></td><td>vv.1-9</td><td>preliminary practice</td></tr>
<tr><td>vv.10-17</td><td>repentance</td></tr>
<tr><td rowspan="3">Ādiyoga nāma samādhi</td><td rowspan="2">lower</td><td>vv.18-54</td><td rowspan="2">purification of practitioner</td></tr>
<tr><td rowspan="5">extant</td><td rowspan="2">Tanaka 1991</td><td>vv.55-65</td></tr>
<tr><td>middle</td><td>vv.66-69</td><td>purification of consort</td></tr>
<tr><td rowspan="5">Maṇḍalarājāgrī nāma samādhi</td><td>Tanaka 1997</td><td>upper</td><td>vv.70-94</td><td>genesis of maṇḍala</td></tr>
<tr><td rowspan="2">Tanaka 2007</td><td rowspan="5"></td><td>vv.95-100</td><td>offering</td></tr>
<tr><td>vv.101-105</td><td rowspan="2">praise</td></tr>
<tr><td rowspan="3">missing</td><td rowspan="3"></td><td>v.106</td></tr>
<tr><td>vv.107-108</td><td>offering of five ambrosia</td></tr>
<tr><td>Karmarājāgrī nāma samādhi</td><td>vv.109-165</td><td></td></tr>
</table>

Guhyasamāja-Mañjuvajra-maṇḍala (Tshatshapuri Gompa) ©Fujita archives

『秘密集会』文殊金剛十九尊曼荼羅

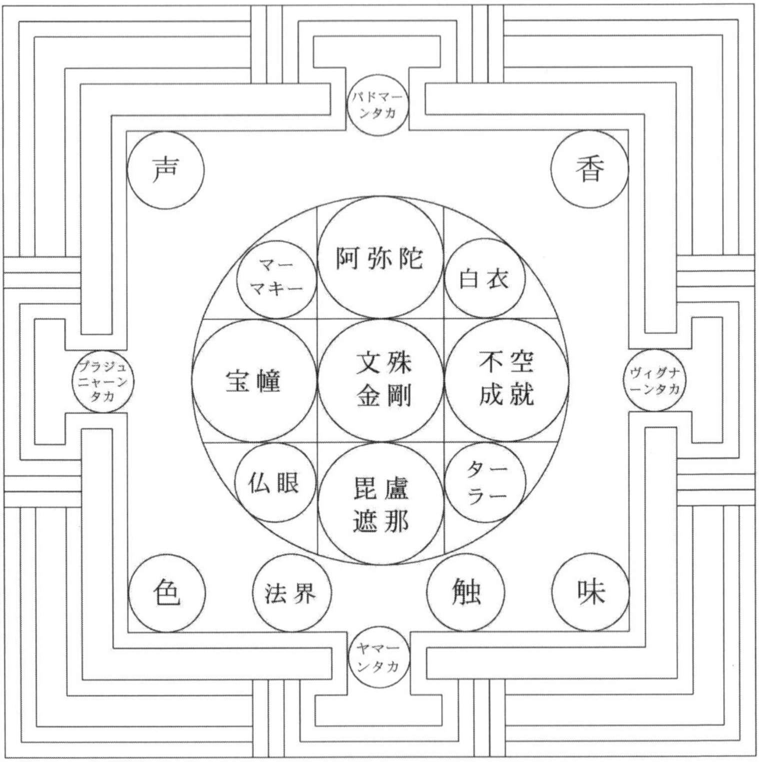

Guhyasamāja-Mañjuvajra-maṇḍala

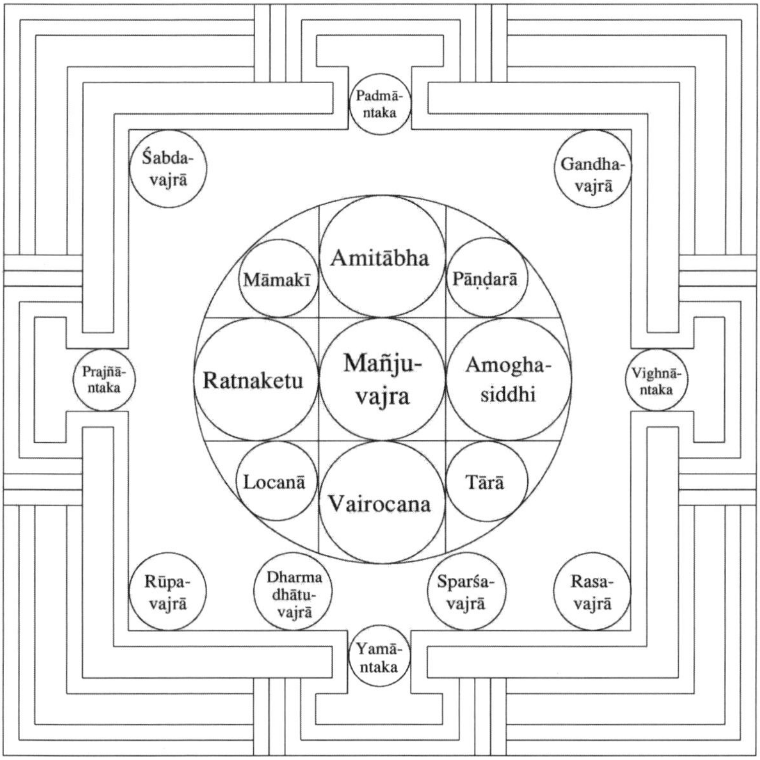

Ādiyoga nāma Samādhi (Sanskrit Commentary)

[na cābhāvo 'pi nirvāṇam][21a1] kuta evāsya bhāvatā/ bhāvābhāva-parāmarṣa[1]kṣayo nirvāṇam ucyata iti// bhagavatāpy uktaṃ/ anirvāṇaṃ hi nirvāṇaṃ lokanāthena deśitaṃ[2]/ ākāśena[3] kṛto granthir ākāśenai[21a2]va[4] mocita iti/ tad iyatā sevā nāma prathamam aṅgaṃ hetusadṛśa[5]devatākhyaṃ mṛduniṣyandaphalam uktam//

Rin chen bzaṅ po's translation:
de 'og raṅ sñiṅ[6] sa bon 'od rnams kyis/
raṅ gi mig sogs sa sñiṅ la sogs pas/
ji bźin bkaṅ nas dri med raṅ zla yis/
rdo rje lte ba'i dbus gnas yi ge Hūṃ//55//

Smṛti's translation:
de 'og gźi yi sa bon 'od kyis[7] ji ltar raṅ la gaṅ ste mig sogs rnams/
sa sñiṅ la sogs dri med raṅ sñiṅ zla ba'i rdo rje bum pa'i dkyil gnas pa//55//

---

1. Ms.: parāmarsa.
2. Ms.: desitam.
3. Ms.: ākāsena.
4. Ms.: ākāsenaiva.
5. Ms.: sadṛsa.
6. P.: sñiṅ po.
7. N.: kyi.

Ādiyoga nāma Samādhi (English Translation)

"Nirvāṇa is not non-existence. [But] how[, equally,] is it existence? Nirvāṇa means the cessation of reference to [both] existence and non-existence."[8] The Lord [Buddha] too has conveyed this, saying: "The Protector of the World has taught that Nirvāṇa is non-Nirvāṇa. A knot made of space is released through space itself."[9] So up to this point, [the author] has explained the first of the [four] limbs [of the *sādhana*], namely, Service (*sevā*). This is termed the Cause-like Deity and its effect is lower *niṣyanda*.

After that, with the flames of their seed[-syllables], one should fill
One's eyes and so forth with [Bodhisattvas] beginning with Kṣitigarbha.[10]
On one's stainless heart-moon, [one should visualise]
The syllable *Hūṃ* in the navel of a thunderbolt. (v. 55)

8. Cited from the *Ratnāvalī*. See Vaidya 1960: 229.

9. Regarding this verse, see Apple 2016.

10. Regarding the point that Bodhisattvas beginning with Kṣitigarbha are assigned to the six sense organs, see Chakravarti 1984: 14–17; Wayman 1977: 10.

//dvitīyam aṅgam āha/ **tadanv** (de 'og) ity adhiṣṭhānānantaram. **nija**[21a3] **bījabhābhir** (raṅ sñiṅ sa bon 'od rnams kyis) iti Kṣitigarbhādīnāṃ ṣaṇṇāṃ bījair yathākramaṃ Kṣiṃkārādibhiś[11] cakṣurādisthāneṣu svasvacihnavaraṭaka-sthitaiḥ/ teṣām eva bhābhiś[12] ca tair eva saprabhair ity arthaḥ/ tad eva[21a4]n nijabījabhābhir hetubhir niṣpannā ye **Kṣitigarbhādayaḥ** (Sa sñiṅ la sogs pas)/ ṣaṭ taiś[13] **cakṣurādīny** (mig sogs) **āpūrya**[14] (bkaṅ nas) dhyāyād iti pareṇa sambandhaḥ/ **yathāsvam** (ji bźin) iti cakṣuḥsthāne candrasthacakramadhyasthita-candrastha[21a5]bhāsvatKṣiṃkārajaṃ Kṣitigarbhaṃ śrotrādi[15]sthāneṣu Vajrapāṇyādikaṃ vidhivad bhāvayed ity arthaḥ/

---

11. Ms.: Kṣiṃkārādibhis.

12. Ms.: bhābhis.

13. Ms.: tais.

14. Ms.: āpūrva; SM: mig sogs bkaṅ nas bsgom par bya.

15. Ms.: srotādi.

He [now] explains the second limb. “Then” means immediately after [this] empowerment. [The word] *nijabījabhābhiḥ* [is to be construed as a *dvandva* compound and] means “by means of the seed-syllables of the six [Bodhisattvas] Kṣitigarbha[, Vajrapāṇi, Ākāśagarbha, Lokeśvara, Sarvanīvaraṇaviṣkambhin] and [Samantabhadra, that is to say, with the syllables] Kṣiṃ, Jriṃ, Khaṃ, Gaṃ, Ṣkaṃ and Saṃ respectively, [visualised each] in the centre of its symbol, in the eyes[, the ears, the nose, the tongue, the whole body] and [mind], and also (*ca*) by means of those [syllables visualized] emitting rays of light.” So one should generate the [Bodhisattvas] headed by Kṣitigarbha out of their causes[, that is to say,] “by means of their seed-syllables and the radiances [there of]”; and then, after making them permeate [one’s] eyes[, ears, nose, tongue, body] and [mind], “one should meditate [on them there]” (*dhyāyāt* [56d]). So there is a syntactic bond with the next verse [56] [that being the source of the main verb *dhyāyāt* (“one should meditate”)].

By “each in his proper place” he means as follows. In the position of one’s eyes one should visualize in the prescribed manner a lunar disc, on that a wheel, on the centre of that wheel a[nother] lunar disc, on that a glowing syllable Kṣiṃ, and then Kṣitigarbha generated from that syllable. Likewise one should visualise Vajrapāṇi[, Ākāśagarbha, Lokeśvara, Sarvanīvaraṇaviṣkambhin] and [Samantabhadra] in the ears[, nose, tongue, body] and [consciousness].

anenopasādhanan nāmāṅgaṃ/ sarvajñatālakṣaṇamṛdu{vipāka}vipākaphalam u[21a6]ktam/ cakṣurādīnāṃ viśuddhas[16] tadviṣaye sūkṣmādiviśeṣa[17] parijñānasaṃbhavāt/ amaletyādinā tṛtīyam aṅgam āha// **amale** (dri med) **svahṛdīndau** (raṅ zla) **vajravaraṭakamadhyasthaṃ** (rdo rje lte ba'i dbus gnas) **Hūṃkāreṇa** (yi ge Hūṃ)[21b1]**Cittavajraṃ** (thugs kyi rdo rje) dhyāyād ity arthaḥ/

thugs kyi rdo rje'i de bźin kha daṅ ni/
mgo bor[18] pa dma 'khor lo la gnas pa'i/
Āḥ[19] daṅ Oṃ ni gsuṅ[20] gi rdo rje daṅ/
sku yi rdo rje ñid du bsam par bya//56//

Hūṃ gi thugs kyi rdo rje kha daṅ mgo la pa dma 'khor lo'i dkyil du yaṅ/ Āḥ[21] daṅ phyag 'tshal[22] gñis kyis gsuṅ gi rdo rje sku yi rdo rje'aṅ bsam par bya//56//

---

16. Ms.: visuddhas.

17. Ms.: viṣeṣa.

18. P.: mgon por.

19. P. N.: A.

20. P.: gsuṅs.

21. P. N.: A.

22. D. C.: phyag mtshan.

In this [verse], he has taught the limb termed Preliminary Practice (*upasādhanam*). This bestows omniscience, the lower Fruit of Maturation (*mṛduvipākaphalam*), for its purification of the eyes[, ears, nose, tongue, body and mind] gives rise to supranormal perceptions in their [respective] fields, enabling one, for example, to see what is [otherwise] too minute to be perceived. In the [clause] beginning *amala-*: "(with the syllable *Hūṃ* in the navel of a vajra) on a spotless (lunar disc) one should visualise Cittavajra in the centre of a vajra on a lunar disc in one's heart by [generating him from] the characters *Hūṃ*, *Āḥ* and *Oṃ*. "One's stainless heart-moon" means that "from the syllable *Hūṃ* on the navel of the multitudinous rays to which he refers are [the products] of these syllables [rather than of the visualized deities]."

Cittavajra. Likewise,
One should meditate on Vāgvajra and Kāyavajra:
The character *Āḥ* on a lotus on the mouth and
The holy syllable on a wheel on the head [respectively]. (v. 56)

vadanaśirasā[23](kha daṅ mgo bor) yathākramaṃ ye **kamalacakre** (pa dma 'khor lo la) tasya nābhau madhyabhāge Āḥkāreṇa **Vāgvajraṃ** (gsuṅ gi rdo rje daṅ)/ praṇava Oṃkāras tena **Kāyavajraṃ** (sku yi rdo rje) **dhyāyād** (bsam par bya) iti sambandhaḥ

de yi thugs ka'i[24] 'od kyi tshogs rnams daṅ/
śes rab dam par gnas pa'i 'od rnams kyis/
kun nas rgyal ba'i dbaṅ po mchod nas ni/
thugs kyi rdo rje la sogs byin gyis brlab//57//

de thugs 'od zer rgyun gyis raṅ gi śes rab daṅ sbyor snaṅ bas kun tu ni/
rgyal ba'i dbaṅ po rnams la mchod nas thugs kyi rdo rje la sogs byin gyis brlab//57//

teṣāṃ (de yi)[21b2]Cittavajrādīnāṃ **hṛdayāni** (thugs ka) teṣāṃ/ **raśmi**[25]**nivahāḥ** ('od kyi tshogs rnams)/ iha hi taddhṛdayeṣu candrasthavajrapadmacakrasthā yathākramaṃ Hūṃ Āḥ Oṃkārā draṣṭavyāḥ/ teṣāṃ raśmi[26]nivahā ity arthaḥ/

---

23. Ms.: sirasā.

24. P. N.: kha'i.

25. Ms.: rasmi.

26. Ms.: rasmi.

One should meditate—this "*dhyāyāt*" connects this verse with the verb in the next verse (*iti sambandhaḥ*)—on Vāgvajra (i.e., Amitābha) with the syllable *Āḥ* and Kāyavajra (i.e., Vairocana) with "*praṇava*," namely, the syllable *Oṃ*, in the centres (*nābhau<madhyabhāge*) of the lotus and wheel, [visualized] in the mouth and head respectively.

Offering to the Kings of Victors (i.e., Buddhas) in all directions,
[One should] empower Cittavajra and others
With the multitudes of rays from their hearts,
And the lights [of uniting] with the excellent consorts. (v. 57)

"Their" means of the [deities] beginning with Cittavajra, "hearts." And their heaps of lights. In this context, one should contemplate on their hearts the syllables *Hūṃ*, *Āḥ* and *Oṃ* on the thunderbolt, lotus and wheel, respectively, on the moon-discs, and their "multitudes of rays."

tais **sa**[21b3]**tprajñāsaṅgabhāsibhiḥ** (śes rab dam par gnas pa'i 'od rnams kyis)/ mayūkhamukhanirgataRūpavajrādipūjādevī[27]rūpaiḥ **parito** (kun nas) daśadigavasthitān **jinendrān** (rgyal ba'i dbaṅ po) **saṃpūjya** (mchod nas ni) tair eva jinendraiḥ pūjitaiḥ/ satprājñāsaṅgabhā[21b4]sibhiḥ/ paścād iti cittavajradharaḥ śrīmān ityādikrameṇa **Cittavajrādīn adhitiṣṭhet** (thugs kyi rdo rje la sogs byin gyis brlab)/

cittavajradharaḥ śrīmāṃs trivajrābhedyabhāvinaḥ/
adhiṣṭhānapadaṃ me 'dya karotu cittavajriṇaḥ//58//
(= *Guhyasamāja* XII,74)

trivajrābhedyabhāvina iti trivajrakāyavajrādi tadabhedabhāvitas tatsvabhāva [21b5]ity arthaḥ/

daśadiksaṃsthitā buddhās trivajrābhedyabhāvitāḥ/
adhiṣṭhānapadaṃ me 'dya kurvantu cittasambhavāḥ//59//
(= *Guhyasamāja* XII,75)

27. Ms.: daivī.

"By them, shining with the excellent consorts" means "in the offering goddesses' forms, Rūpavajrā and so on, born from the tip of the ray," and "in all directions" means the "Kings of Victors (Buddhas)" dwelling in ten directions are offered. By them, namely, nobody other than the offered Kings of Victors, shining with the excellent consorts. "After" means by the sequence beginning with [the verse] *Cittavajradhara śrīmān* (i.e., v. 58 or *Guhyasamāja* XII,74), one should contemplate Cittavajra and others.

O glorious holder of the adamantine mind,
You who are practising the three vajras inseparably!
Please empower me,
So as to achieve the state of the mind-vajra! (v. 58)

Verse 58 (*trivajrābhedyabhāvina*[28] *iti*). "The three vajras" means Kāyavajra and so on [= body, speech and mind vajras]. "Practising them inseparably" means [the one whose] nature is such.

No comment on Verse 59.

28. I have adopted *trivajrābhedyabhāvinaḥ* in accordance with the Sanskrit commentary, although Matsunaga 1978 has *trivajrābhedyabhāvitaḥ*.

Oṃ sarvatathāgatacittavajrasvabhāvātmako 'haṃ

dharmo vai vākpathaḥ śrīmāṃs trivajrābhedyabhāvitaḥ/
adhiṣṭhānapadaṃ me 'dya karotu vākyavajriṇaḥ//60//
(= *Guhyasamāja* XII,72)

dharmo Vāgvajraḥ[/] **vākpatha** iti vacanasthāpanopapannaḥ/ śeṣan[29] tu prasiddham eva/

daśadiksaṃsthitā buddhās trivajrābhedyabhāvitāḥ/
adhiṣṭhānapadaṃ tasya kurvantu vākpathodbhavam//61//
(= *Guhyasamāja* XII,73)

Oṃ sarvatathāgatavāgvajrasvabhāvātmako 'haṃ

buddhakāyadharaḥ śrīmāṃs trivajrābhedyabhāvitaḥ/
adhiṣṭhānapadaṃ me 'dya karotu kāyavajriṇaḥ//62//
(= *Guhyasamāja* XII,70)

daśadiksaṃsthitā buddhās trivajrābhedyabhāvitāḥ/
adhiṣṭhānapadaṃ me 'dya kurvantu kāyalakṣitam//63//
(= *Guhyasamāja* XII,71)

---

29. Ms.: seṣan.

Oṃ sarvatathāgatacittavajrasvabhāvātmako 'haṃ.

O glorious Dharma, pathway of speech!
You who are practising the three vajras inseparably!
Please empower me,
So as to achieve the state of the speech-vajra! (v. 60)

"Dharma" means Vāgvajra (i.e., Amitābha). Pathway of speech (*vākpatha*)[30] means the appearance of the fixed meaning of the word. The others are well known [and need not be explained].

No comment on Verse 61.

No comment on Verse 62.

No comment on Verse 63.

30. Matsunaga 1978 has *vaivākpatha*.

Oṃ sarvatathāgatakāyavajrasvabhāvātmako 'haṃ

nam mkha' lta bu'i[31] ṅo bor rdo rje gsum/
mtshan ñid dag daṅ bral bar dmigs nas ni/
phyogs bcur kun du bźugs pa'i[32] thub pa'i tshogs/
sñiṅ po'i 'od zer rnams kyis yaṅ dag bskul//64//

rdo rje gsum ni nam mkha'i raṅ bźin mtshan ma spaṅs pa mtshon byas te/ sems kyi 'od zer rnams kyis bskul nas thams cad tshogs su gyur pa'i thub pa'i sde//64//

tato gāthāmantrair adhiṣṭhitasyāsya trivajrasya viśuddhirūpatām ākhyātum āha// [21b6]gaganopametyādi/ grāhyādi**lakṣaṇāpagata**(mtshan ñid dag daṅ bral bar)tvād eva **gaganopamasvabhāvaṃ** (nam mkha' lta bu'i ṅo bor) śūnyatā[33] rūpam idaṃ **trivajraṃ** (rdo rje gsum) draṣṭavyam ity arthaḥ/ tad itthaṃ trivajraṃ viśuddha[34]rūpam āla[kṣya] sva[ku][22a1]lodbhāsimauliḥ syād iti pareṇa sambandhaḥ/ iyatā tu sādhanan nāmāṅgaṃ// dharmmasambhoga-nirmmāṇalakṣaṇakāyatritayaviśuddhi[35]rūpamṛdupuruṣakāraphalam uktaṃ/ Cittavajrādīnāṃ yathā[22a2]kramaṃ [dharma]kāyādirūpatvāt//

31. P. N.: bur.

32. P.: kun bźugs pa yi.

33. Ms.: sūnyatā.

34. Ms.: visuddha.

35. Ms.: visuddhi.

Oṃ sarvatathāgatakāyavajrasvabhāvātmako 'haṃ.

Visualizing the three vajras whose nature is like space
And free of [all] characteristics,
One should invoke, with the lights of the heart,
The Buddhas assembled in ten directions. (v. 64)

In order to declare the purity of these three vajras that have been empowered by verses and mantras (i.e., verses 61–63), he said "like space" and so on. The meaning is that these three vajras, whose nature is emptiness, are to be seen as being like space in their nature for the reason that they lack the characteristics of the object of perception and so on (= *grāhya-grāhaka*).

The connection with the next verse is as follows: when he has recognized the three vajras as having their nature purified in this way, "he will become one whose crown is radiant with his clan[-deity]."

Up to this point, [he has] explained the limb named *sādhana*, which is the lower *Puruṣakāra-phala* and has the form of purity of three bodies, namely, Dharma, Sambhoga and Nirmāṇa. It should be Cittavajra = *dharmakāya*; Vāgvajra = *sambhogakāya*; and Kāyavajra = *nirmāṇakāya*.

//caturtham aṅgam āha/ saṃcodyety ādi/ iha khalu Cittavajrādiniṣpādanavelāyām eva CittaVāgvajrayor antarāle jñānasatvo bhagavān samayasa[22a3]ttvarūpī candrasthakhaḍga[36]muṣṭimadhyasthacandre niṣaṇṇo draṣṭavyas[37] tasya **hṛtprabhābhiḥ** (sñiṅ po'i 'od zer rnams kyis) **sakalākāśa**[38]**valayavarttimuni-vṛndam** (phyogs bcur kun du bźugs pa'i thub pa'i tshogs) iti sarvadiksamūha-sthitaṃ/ sugatanivahaṃ **saṃcodya** (yaṅ dag bskul)

thub pa'i mchog gi 'od zer las byuṅ ba'i/
rig pa'i tshogs rnams phyag na bum bsnams te/
ye śes chu yis mṅon par dbaṅ bskur bas/
raṅ gi rigs kyi gtsos brgyan cod pan gyur//65//

thub mchog 'od zer las byuṅ rig ma'i[39] tshogs kyi yaṅ dag 'dzin pa yi/
bum pa'i ye śes chu yis blugs pas raṅ rig gtso bo snaṅ bas dbu brgyan gyur//65//

---

36. Ms.: khadga.

37. Ms.: draṣṭavya.

38. Ms.: sakalākāsa.

39. P. N.: ma.

[Next,] he has stated the fourth limb [in the passage] beginning "Send forth." In this context, at the very moment Cittavajra and others are born, between Cittavajra and Vāgvajra, one should contemplate Bhagavat *jñānasattva* [Knowlege-being] in the form of the *samayasattva* [Pledge-being] sitting on the moon-disc between a sword and a fist on the moon-discs. "With the rays from his hearts," [one should] send forth the assembly of the Munis until they are in multitudes in all directions.

[Once the recipient] has been empowered with the water of wisdom
From the pots held by the assemblage of goddesses (*vidyā*)
Who are born from the rays of supreme Munis,
The radiance of the chief of his family becomes his diadem. (v. 65)

teṣām[40] [22a4]saṃcoditānāṃ **munivarāṇāṃ** (thub pa'i mchog gi) **marīcibhyo** ('od zer las) **nirgatā** (byuṅ ba'i) ye **vidyāgaṇā** (rig pa'i tshogs rnams) Rūpavajrādayas teṣāṃ **karaiḥ** (phyag na) **samuddhṛtā** (bsnams te) ye jñānapūrṇṇāḥ[41] **kalaśās**[42] (bum) taiḥ kalaśair[43] **jñānāmbv** (ye śes chu yis) **abhiṣiktaḥ**[44] (mṅon par dbaṅ bskur) san/ Ma[22a5]ñjuvajrātmayogī **svakulodbhāsimauliḥ syāt** (raṅ gi rigs kyi gtsos brgyan cod pan gyur)/ asya svakuleśo[45] 'kṣobhyas tenoddīpitamaulir bhavet/ abhiṣekānantaraṃ Mañjuśrī[46]makuṭe Akṣobhyo draṣṭavya ity[47] arthaḥ//[22a6]anena mahāsādhanam aṅgam abhiṣekarūpamṛduvaimalyaphalam uktaṃ/ jñānodakābhiṣekeṇa vaimalyāyārdanāt/ tad evaṃ sevādīni catvāry aṅgāni[48] pradhānadevatā[22b1]gatatvād uttamaśabdaviśeṣaṇāni[49] sakalavipakṣāpanayanāśaktatvenā[50]paṭutvān mṛdūni yathāsvaṃ phalayuktāny uktāni/

---

40. Ms.: teṣāma.

41. After writing *jñānāpūrṇṇa*, the scribe revised it to *jñānapūrṇṇa*.

42. Ms.: kalasās.

43. Ms.: kalasair.

44. *jñānāmbu*[']*bhiṣiktaḥ* is ungrammatical. It should be *jñānāmbvabhiṣiktaḥ*. In this Ms. such irregular liaison also occurs in note 48.

45. Ms.: kuleso.

46. Ms.: Mañjusrī.

47. After writing *draṣṭavyaḥ*, the scribe changed visarga to the character "i."

48. Ms.: angani.

49. Ms.: viseṣaṇāni.

50. Ms.: sakalavipakṣāpanayanāsaktatvena.

The assemblage of the goddesses beginning with Rūpavajrā is born from the rays of the supreme Munis sent forth [by the Knowledge-being]. And having pots full of wisdom in their hands, they pour over [the recipient] the water of wisdom. [Now,] the yogi, becoming Mañjuvajra, will have his diadem shining with his clan. The chief of Mañjuvajra's own clan is Akṣobhya, and therefore the diadem will shine with Akṣobhya. This means that immediately after initiation, [one should] contemplate Akṣobhya on Mañjuśrī's diadem.

In this [verse], the limb named *mahāsādhana*, [which has] the form of initiation and [is also] lower *vaimalya-phala*, has been explained. It is called "*vaimalya*" because initiation with the water of wisdom produces stainlessness. So, in this way, he has explained the four limbs beginning with *sevā* with their respective effects (*phala*). They are characterized by the term "supreme" because they occur in the main deity, and are said to be "lower" because they are not intense, [and that is] because they are unable to remove all the opponents.

de bźin raṅ gi lha 'dra raṅ sñiṅ pos/
sprul pa'i rig pa ñid ni yaṅ dag blta[51]/
mig la sogs pa dgaṅ źiṅ ye śes gsum/
rnam par bkod pas lus ni 'od daṅ ldan//66//

de bźin raṅ gi lha mo 'dra bar raṅ gi sñiṅ po'aṅ bsgoms nas rig mar sprul/
mig la sogs pa gaṅ nas yig 'bru gsum bkod 'bar ba'i lus ldan ma//66//

idānīm aparāṇi catvāri sevā niṣyandādīni/[22b2]prajñāviśodhanāni[52]/ mṛdu['] dhimātrayoś[53] caturaṃgayor[54] mmadhyavarttitvān madhyaśabdaviśeṣa[55]ṇāny āha/ **tadvad** (de bźin) iti/ Mañjuvajravat sevādikrameṇa **vidyāṃ** (rig pa) **saṃvīkṣya** (yaṅ dag blta) tatvajño mantrī [22b3] sugatān anurāgayāmīty adhimokṣeṇa tayā saha ratim ārabhed iti sambandhaḥ/ tāny eva sevādīni darśayan vidyām viśinaṣṭi [56]/ **svahṛde**(raṅ sñiṅ pos)ti Mañjuvajrabījena **nirmitāṃ** (sprul pa)/ **sva**[22b4] **devatābhām** (raṅ gi lha 'dra) iti/ Mañjuvajrākārā/ ete nyasyāḥ sevā[/] madhyaniṣyandaphalāḥ sūcitāḥ/

51. P. N.: lta.

52. Ms.: visodhanāni.

53. See note 39.

54. Ms.: caturaṃgayos.

55. Ms.: madhyasabdavisesa.

56. Ms.: visinaṣṭi.

[One should] contemplate a goddess in the likeness of oneself as the deity,
Emanated from one's own heart.
Having filled the eyes and [the other sense-organs] and adorned her with three syllables, her body will be radiant. (v. 66)

Now [he] has explained the next set of four limbs beginning with *sevā-niṣyanda*, those which purify the consort (*prajñāviśodhana*) and are termed "medium" because they are between the lower and higher sets, [in the verse beginning with the words] "In his likeness (*tadvat*)." The sentence is completed as follows [supplying the subject and verb from verses 67 and 69]: Contemplating the goddess (*vidyā*) in the likeness of Mañjuvajra, the practitioner "who knows the truth" should begin to make love to her with the conviction that he is pleasuring the Sugatas.

Proceeding to explain this [sequence] beginning with *sevā*, he defines the goddess as emanated in the likeness of his deity from his "heart," from the Mañjuvajra seed[-syllable], that is to say, in the likeness of Mañjuvajra. In this [verse] he has alluded to her *sevā* with medium *niṣyanda-phala*.

āpūrṇṇacakṣurādyām (mig la sogs pa dgaṅ źiṅ) iti/ tadvad eva svabīja-niṣpannaiḥ Kṣitigarbhādibhir niṣpā[22b5]ditacakṣurādi- ṣaṭkāmenopasādhanaṃ madhyamavipākaphalaṃ sūcitaṃ tryakṣaraṃ (yi ge gsum)/ Hūṃ Āḥ Oṃkārās teṣāṃ pūrvadevacittavajrādirūpeṇa pūrvoktasthāneṣu dhyānaṃ **vinyāsaṃ** (rnam par bkod pas)[22b6]etena sādhanaṃ madhyapuruṣakāraphalaṃ sūcitaṃ/ tadanantaraṃ pūrvadevajñānodakābhiṣekā- dinā bhāsvaraṃ nirmmalaśarīraṃ[57] yasyāḥ sā akṣara**vinyāsabhāsva[raśarī]rā** (rnam par bkod pas lus ni 'od daṅ ldan)[23a1] etena mahāsādhanam madhya- vaimalyaphalaṃ sūcitaṃ/

de ñid śes pas mgo daṅ sñiṅ ga daṅ/
lte ba gsaṅ ba de bźin brla gñis sogs/
Oṃ Hūṃ Svā Āḥ Hā źes grags pa rnams/
de ni sku thugs rdo rje bzaṅ rigs sogs//67//

'og sñiṅ lte ba gsaṅ ba de bźin brla gñis sogs la de ñid śes par bya/
Oṃ Hūṃ Svā Āḥ Hā źes bya bas[58] lus yid rdo rje dam pa'i rigs tshogs kyis[59] //67//

57. Ms.: sarīraṃ.

58. P. N.: byas pas.

59. P. N.: kyi.

[He also describes her as] "filling the eyes and [the other sense-organs]." By [referring in this way to] the six sensual objects of the eye and [other organs] which have been perfected by [the six Bodhisattvas] beginning with Kṣitigarbha who had been created like him (i.e., Mañjuvajra) from their respective syllables, this alludes to [her] *upasādhana* with medium *vipāka- phala*. The "three syllables" are *Hūṃ Āḥ Oṃ*. Their meditation, [that is to say,] their disposition (*vinyāsa*), is [to be] in the form of [the] above-mentioned [three deities] beginning with Cittavajra on the aforesaid points [in her body].

This alludes to [her] *sādhana* with medium *puruṣakāra-phala*. Immediately after this, her body becomes radiant and stainless through the aforesaid sequence of initiations beginning with that with the water of divine wisdom; and so she is [indeed] "adorned with three syllables and her body radiant." This [last expression] alludes to [her] *mahāsādhana* with medium *vaimalya-phala*.

With wisdom of truth, one [should visualize]
Syllables called *Oṃ*, *Hūṃ*, *Svā*, *Āḥ* and *Hā* [respectively]
On the head, heart, navel, private parts and both thighs and so forth.
They are the excellent clans of adamantine body, mind and the rest. (v. 67)

tām evaṃbhūtāṃ pañcakulakalāpinītvena viśinaṣṭi[60]/ **śirasi**[61] **hṛdi** (mgo daṅ sñiṅ ga) **nābhau** (lte ba) **guhye** (gsaṅ ba)/ **ūruyugmādike** (brla gñis sogs) ca/ yathākramam/ Oṃ Hūṃ Svā [23a2] Āḥ Hā ity etair bījai[r] niṣpāditāni[62] yāni **kāyamanovajrasatkulādyāni** (sku thugs rdo rje bzaṅ rigs sogs) kāyavajrarūpaṃ satkulan tathāgatakulaṃ/ evam manovajrasatkula[ṃ] vajrakulaṃ/ ādyaśabdād ra [23a3]tnakulam/ padmakulaṃ karmmakulaṃ ca gṛhyate/

lha po rnams kyis yan lag byin brlabs te/
'od kyi phreṅ ba dam pas 'gro gsum khyab/
Āḥ[63] yis sna tshogs pa dma'i lte ba bya/
Hūṃ gis 'dab ma brgyad pa rnam par sprul//68//

de lha'i byin brlabs lus ni 'gro gsum khyab pas dam pa'i 'od tshogs bsam/
Āḥs bskyed rnam par bkod pa'i sñiṅ po Hūṃ las sprul pa'i pad ma 'dab brgyad pa//68//

60. Ms.: visinaṣṭi.

61. Ms.: sirasi.

62. Ms.: niṣpādaitāni.

63. P. N.: A.

Now that she has arisen in this form (*evambhūtām*), he describes (*viśinaṣṭi*) her (*tām*) as comprising the totality of [all] the five clans [*pañcakula-kalāpinītva*]. The "excellent clans [*satkula*] of adamantine body, mind and the rest" are perfected with these [five] syllables, namely, *Oṃ Hūṃ Svā Āḥ* and *Hā*, respectively, "on (1) her head, (2) her heart, (3) her navel, (4) her private parts, and (5) her thighs and so forth." [Of these] the "excellent clan whose nature is the adamantine body" is the Tathāgata clan. Likewise, that of the adamantine mind is the Vajra clan. "The rest" refers to the [remaining three] clans[, namely, those] of Padma, Ratna and Karma.

[The goddess] whose body was empowered with these five [syllables]
Attains a perfect halo that expands to pervade the triple universe.
[One should contemplate] the pericarp of a multi-coloured lotus from the
syllable *Āḥ* and create eight petals from the syllable *Hūṃ*. (v. 68)

taiḥ **pañcabhir** (lṅa po rnams kyis) yathākramaṃ **adhiṣṭhitāṅgī** (yan lag byin brlabs te) **jagattrayavyāpi** ('gro gsum khyab) **satprabhāvalayām**[64] ('od kyi phreṅ ba dam pas) iti/ traidhātukavyāpisphuratkaranikarām/ **Āḥ**[23a4]**kāreṇa** (Āḥ yis) **kṛtavicitrakarṇṇikaś** (sna tshogs pa dma'i lte ba bya) ca/ **Hūṃkāreṇa** (Hūṃ gis) **vinirmitāṣṭadalaś** ('dab ma brgyad pa rnam par sprul) ca kamalaṃ yasyāḥ sā tathoktāṃ/

śes rab dam pa'i rgyu mthun ṅo bo ñid/
thabs daṅ bcas par 'byuṅ[65] ba'i raṅ gi lus/
de yis[66] bde gśegs rjes su mñes bya źes/
sṅags pas dga' ba kun tu brtsam par bya//69//

pa dma'i śes rab rgyu mthun raṅ bźin thabs daṅ bcas par gyur pa'i gźi yi[67] lus bsṅags pa/
de daṅ lhan cig bde gśegs rnams la rjes su chags par bgyi źes brtsams//69//

---

64. Tib. suggests *prabhāvalyāṃ*.

65. P.: 'gyur.

66. P.: yi.

67. P. N.: gyur pa yi gźi'i.

Once "her body has been empowered by these five [syllables]" [placed] in order [at the said locations], she manifests a radiant (*-sat-<-sphurat-*) mass (*-valayām<-nikarām*) of rays (*-prabhā-<-kara-*) that expands to pervade (*vyāpi*) the triple universe (*jagattraya-<traidhātuka-*). She is [also] described as having a lotus (i.e., vagina) with a multi-coloured pericarp created out of the syllable *Āḥ* and eight petals created out of the syllable *Hūṃ*.

The practitioner
Whose nature is flowing forth excellent wisdom (i.e., female consort)
And has his own body born in posession of the means (i.e., male consort)
Should be pleasuring the Sugatas and begin to make love in this way. (v. 69)

Oṃ sarvatathāgatānurāgaṇavajrasvabhāvātmako 'haṃ

tām īdṛśī[ṃ] saṃvīkṣya kiṃbhūto **ratim ārabhata** (dga' ba kun tu brtsam par bya) ity āha// **satprajñā** (śes rab dam pa) hetu[23a5]janakaVajradharaprajñā/ tan **niṣyandasvabhāvaḥ** (rgyu mthun ṅo bo ñid)/ **sopāyabhūto** (thabs daṅ bcas par 'byuṅ ba'i) **nijadeho** (raṅ gi lus) yasya **mantriṇaḥ** (sṅags pas) sa tathoktaṃ/ vajra[ṃ] mantriṇo Hūṃkāreṇa niṣpādyaṃ/ ata evānantaraṃ vakṣyati/ Hūṃ[23a6]vajranirgatāmalam iti/ anurāgaṇayogādhiṣṭhānamantram āha// Oṃ ityādi// //iyatā grantheṇādiyogo nāma prathama[samādhi][68]niruktaḥ//

68. *samādhi* inserted from margin.

Oṃ sarvatathāgatānurāgaṇavajrasvabhāvātmako 'haṃ.

Next, he has explained the nature that the practitioner should have when, having visualized her in this form, he proceeds to pleasure [her]. [Thus] he describes the practitioner as one whose body personifies the male consort [literally: "one whose body is (*-bhūtaḥ*) with *upāya*"], being of the nature of that which flows forth from "the excellent consort" (*satprajñā*) from the consort of the father, the causal Vajradhara.[69] The thunderbolt of the practitioner (*vajra[ṃ] mantriṇo*) should be generated with the syllable *Hūṃ*, [for] he will refer immediately after this to "the stainless [being] born from the *Hūṃ*[-generated] thunderbolt." [Next] he has stated in the words beginning with *Oṃ* the mantra that empowers [this] Yoga of sexual pleasuring (*anurāgaṇa-*).[70] So far he has explained (*niruktaḥ*) the first *Samādhi*, that which is known as *Ādiyoga*.

69. On causal Vajradhara, see Tanaka 2010: 288–294.

70. This corresponds to the mantra *Oṃ sarvatathāgatānurāgaṇavajrasvabhāvātmako 'haṃ* expounded in *Guhyasamāja* VI.

thugs ka'i zla ba'i sṅags kyi 'od rnams kyis/
ma lus saṅs rgyas tshogs rnams bcug nas ni/
Hūṃ gi rdo rje las byuṅ dri ma med pa yi/
yid tshul dam pa'i chu[71] skyes la gnas pa//70//

sems kyi zla ba'i 'od kyis ma lus saṅs rgyas tshogs ni bźugs gnas te/
Hūṃ gi rdo rjer byuṅ nas dri med pa dma la gnas dam pa'i yid kyi gzugs//70//

[23b1]idānīm aparāṇi catvāri sevāniṣyandādīni sarvadevatā{ṃ}gatatvāt{/} sāmānyāni jñānaviśeṣavaśād[72] adhimātraśabda[73]viśeṣaṇāni[74] vaktuṃ maṇḍalarājāgrīsamādhim utpatti[23b2]krameṇāha/ hṛccandretyādi/

71. P.N.: tshul.

72. Ms.: viseṣavasād.

73. Ms.: sabda.

74. Ms.: viseṣaṇāni.

The Generation of the 19-deity Maṇḍala of Mañjuvajra (English Translation)

With the rays of the mantra on the moon-disc on the heart,
The assemblage of all the Buddhas enters into [the body].
The stainless [being] born from the *Hūṃ*[-generated] thunderbolt,
The form of excellent mind, rests upon the lotus. (v. 70)

Now, in the verse beginning "*hṛccandra-*" he explains (*āha*) the "*Maṇḍala-rājāgrī [nāma] samādhi*" through the process of generation (*utpattikrama*) in order to teach (*vaktum*) the next set of four limbs beginning with *sevā-niṣyanda*, which are called "the ordinary" (*sāmānyāni*) because they apply to all the deities [of this maṇḍala, rather than only to the principal deities, as was the case in the *Ādiyoga*], and "the higher" because of the superiority of knowledge [that they reveal].

jñānasatvahṛccandrasthamuṣṭisthitacandrastho mantro **hṛccandramantraḥ** (thugs ka'i zla ba'i sṅags)/ tasya **bhābhir** ('od rnams kyis) **nniḥśeṣa**[75]**buddha sandohaṃ** (ma lus saṅs rgyas tshogs rnams)/ svaśarīre[76] mukhena **praveśya**[77] (bcug nas ni) **samastanijamāṇḍaleya**[23b3]**rūpeṇa** (ma lus pa'i raṅ gi dkyil 'khor pa yi gzugs) svahṛtprasūtaṃ dhyātvā **lokahitahetoḥ** ('jig rten rnams la phan phyir) **sthiracittaḥ** (sems ni brtan po) **samutsṛjed** (yaṅ dag dbyuṅ) iti sambandhaḥ [/] Hūṃkāreṇa vajraṃ **Hūṃvajraṃ** (Hūṃ gi rdo rje) tanmārgeṇa nirgatañ ca tad **amalañ** (dri ma med pa) ca **sanmanorūpam** (yid tshul dam pa) iti prave[23b4]śita[78]buddhasamūhapariṇāmajaṃ bodhicittaṃ/ **aṃbhoruhavattī** (chu skyes la gnas pa) ti devīkamalodaravarttidhyātvā

raṅ gi sñiṅ po las byuṅ ma lus pa'i/
raṅ gi dkyil 'khor pa yi gzugs bsams la/
cho ga 'di yis sems ni brtan po daṅ/
'jig rten rnams la phan phyir yaṅ dag dbyuṅ//71//

bsams nas raṅ gi sñiṅ pos bskyed pa thams cad gźi yi dkyil 'khor lha gzugs su/ cho ga 'di yi sems ni brtan po daṅ źes pa nas 'jig rten phan pa'i rgyu phyir 'byuṅ bar bya//71//

75. Ms.: nniḥseṣa.

76. Ms.: svasarīre.

77. Ms.: pravesya.

78. M.: prevesita.

By "mantra in the heart-moon" (*hṛccandramantraḥ*) he means the mantra on a moon[-disc visualized] on a fist upon a lotus[-seat] in the heart of the *jñāna-sattva*. With rays [emitted] from it, he should [draw down and] cause to enter his body through his mouth the assembly of all the Buddhas. The sentence is completed as follows [supplying the subject and verb from verse 71]: He should meditate on them as [re-]emerging (*prasūtaṃ*) from his heart as all the surrounding deities proper to [the Mañjuvajra-]maṇḍala, and then, with unwavering awareness, he should emit them for the benefit of [all] sentient beings.

By "the *Hūṃ*-thunderbolt" he means "the thunderbolt [generated] by [the syllable] *Hūṃ*." By "that whose form is supreme (*sat-*) awareness (*manaḥ*), pure and flowing out (*nirgatam*) through that (*tanmārgeṇa*)," he refers to the Bodhicitta (i.e., semen) that is the product of metamorphosis of all the Buddhas whom he has caused to enter it. [When he says that it rests] "in the lotus" he means [that it rests] in the heart of the lotus (i.e., vagina) of the goddess.

One should meditate on all the surrounding deities of the maṇḍala
Born from his own heart.
In this way, the one with unwavering awareness
Should emit [them] for the benefit of the triple universe. (v. 71)

svahṛtprasūtam (raṅ gi sñiṅ po las byuṅ) iti/ svahṛd yathokto Maṃkāro/ tatpariṇatakrameṇa **samastanija**[23b5]**māṇḍaleyadevatārūpeṇ**(ma lus pa'i raṅ gi dkyil 'khor pa yi gzugs)otpannaṃ tad eva bodhicittam īdṛśaṃ[79] **dhyātvā** (bsams la) iti vakṣyamāṇena **vidhinā samutsṛjet** (cho ga 'di yis...yaṅ dag dbyuṅ)/ kūṭāgāra[ṃ] maṇḍale sthāpayituṃ yogī devīkamalodarā[24a1]n niścārayed[80] ity arthaḥ/ yad uktaṃ/ prathamaṃ śūnyatā[81]bodhi[ṃ] dvitīyaṃ bījasaṃgrahaṃ/ tṛtīyaṃ bimbaniṣpatti[ś] caturthaṃ nyāsam akṣaram iti/ tam eva kamalotpannadevatācakro[tsa]rga[24a2]vidhim āha/

vajradhṛk ces bya daṅ thugs rdo rje/
skye bo dam pa'i don mdzad yaṅ dag bskul/
nor bu sṅon po'i 'od 'drar yaṅ dag 'bar/
g-yas daṅ g-yon pa'i źal ni dkar daṅ dmar//72//

va dzra drik ces bskul nas thugs kyi rdo rje 'gro ba'i don mchog byed pa ni/ g-yas g-yon źal ni dkar dmar 'bar ba'i mthiṅ ga dam pa nor bu 'dra ba'i mdog//72//

79. M.: īdṛsaṃ.

80. M.: niscārayed.

81. M.: sūnyatā.

In the verses beginning with "Born from his own heart," "his own heart" means the syllable *Maṃ* that was explained above. "In this way" (*iti vidhinā*), that is to say, in the manner that will be stated presently (*vakṣyamāṇena*), he should emit this same Bodhicitta [only] after he has meditated upon it as having this nature (*īdṛśaṃ*), [that is to say,] as having been transformed into (*-rūpeṇotpannaṃ*) all the [surrounding] deities proper to the [Mañjuvajra-] maṇḍala through (*-krameṇa*) the metamorphosis (*-pariṇati* [em.]) of this [syllable]. It is implied (*ity arthaḥ*) that the yogi should generate the celestial mansion from the heart of the lotus of the goddess.

This is confirmed [by the *Guhyasamāja*] when it says: "First, realization of emptiness; second, the absorption into the seed[-syllable]; third, the creation of the [deities'] form; and fourth, the disposition of the syllables."[82] In this verse, [the *Guhyasamāja*] has explained the same process of generating the circle of deities from the lotus [of the goddess].

He should provoke Vajradhṛk, namely, Cittavajra,
The supreme benefactor of sentient beings,
Whose [main face and body] are radiant like sapphire,
And right and left [faces] are white and red [respectively]. (v. 72)

---

82. *Guhyasamāja* XIII,138. However, Matsunaga adopted *bījasaṃhṛtam* instead of *bījasaṃgrahaṃ* in pāda B.

saṃcodyetyādi/ **cittavajram** (thugs rdo rje) Akṣobhya yathānirddiṣṭa{/} viśeṣānvitaṃ[83]/

dam pa daṅ po lta bu'i phyag daṅ ldan/
kha dog dpag tu med pa'i 'od tshogs mṅa'/
blo daṅ ldan pas legs bsdus bdag ñid kyi/
dṅos po thams cad kyis ni źugs par bya//73//

mchog gi daṅ po bźin du phyag daṅ ldan pa du ma'i mdog gis 'od kyis tshogs/ 'dus nas bdag la blo daṅ ldan pas dṅos po kun gyis thim par bya//73//

paramādyavadbhujānvitam (dam pa daṅ po lta bu'i phyag daṅ ldan) iti vajrasatvavadbhujaiḥ/ kuliśāsi[84]kamalamaṇidha[24a3]rair anvitaṃ/ vajradhṛg ity utsargamantreṇa saṃcodya **saṃhṛtavye**(legs bsdus)ti{/} vipañcita[s]pharaṇādy-ākārasaṃhāreṇānīya **sarvabhāvena** (dṅos po thams cad kyis ni) sarvātmenā ātmani Mañjuśrī[85]rūpe **nive**[24a4]**śayet**[86](źugs par bya) / **dhīmān** (blo daṅ ldan pas) iti niveśyaniveśaka[87]graharahitaḥ/

83. M.: viseṣānvitaṃ.

84. M.: kulisāsi.

85. Ms.: Mañjusrī.

86. Ms.: nivesayet.

87. Ms.: nivesyanivesaka.

[Now, the verse] beginning "He should provoke." The "Cittavajra" [that he should provoke] is Akṣobhya with the characteristics explained [in this verse].

[Akṣobhya] has hands like Paramādya's
[And] also has multi-coloured rays.
With wisdom, one should contract oneself
And enter into [the deity] with complete devotion. (v. 73)

"With hands like Paramādya's"[88] means with hands holding a thunderbolt, sword, lotus and jewel [respectively] like Vajrasattva. One should arouse [Akṣobhya] with "*Vajradhṛk*," the mantra of emission. "Having contracted" (*saṃhṛtya* [em.]), [that is to say,] having gathered and drawn in (*-saṃhāreṇānīya*) the manifold rays that have emanated, the [yogi] should merge them completely (*sarvabhāvena<sarvātmanā*) into himself as Mañjuśrī, [doing so] with wisdom (*dhīmān*), [that is to say,] without clinging to the [false belief] that there is a [real] agent or a [real] object in this act of merging.

88. *Paramādya* is the title of a yoga-tantra that developed from the *Prajñāpāramitānaya-sūtra*. However, in this case it means Vajrasattva as the primordial Buddha explained in this tantra.

ji na jik ces bya ba sku rdo rje/
rdo rje 'dzin 'dra'i[89] sku mdog źal gyis mdzes/
'khor lo la sogs phyag mtshan rnams de bźin/
śar gyi pa dmar zla ba'i dbus su bsam//74//

ji na jik ces bskul ba'i rdo rje 'dzin ltar mdog daṅ źal sogs ldan/
śar gyi zla ba pad ma'i dbus su 'khor sogs mtshan pa de bźin bsam//74//

kāyavajraṃ (sku rdo rje) Vairocanaṃ yathoktaviśeṣaṇañ[90] **cakrādicihnam** ('khor lo la sogs phyag mtshan rnams) iti cakrakhadgapadmamaṇibhi[r] lakṣitaṃ/ **tadvad** (de bźin) iti citta[24a5]vajravaj jinajig ity utsargamantreṇa saṃcodya **pūrvakamalendumadhye dhyāyāt** (śar gyi pa dmar zla ba'i dbus su bsam)/

ra tna dhṛg ces bya ba 'di yis ni/
lho ru[91] rin chen 'byuṅ źal gźon nu 'dra/
btso ma'i gser gyi mdaṅs daṅ 'dra ba la/
phyag drug ma rgad rin chen la sogs bsnams//75//

ra tna dhṛk ces lho ru rin chen dbaṅ phyug źal rnams gźon nu'i mdog 'dra ba/
btso ma'i gser daṅ 'dra ba ma rgad rin chen la sogs mdzes pa'i phyag drug pa//75//

89. P. N.: daṅ 'dra ba'i.

90. Ms.: viseṣaṇañ.

91. P. N.: nor bu.

[One should] provoke Kāyavajra with [the mantra] Jinajik.
The colour of his body and faces are like Vajradhara.
[He] holds the symbols beginning with the wheel similar to him.
[One] should contemplate him in the centre of a moon-disc on a lotus in the east. (v. 74)

Kāyavajra is Vairocana with the characteristics explained [in this verse]. [He] holds "the symbols beginning with the wheel," that is to say, he is characterized by a wheel, sword, lotus and jewel. [Vairocana] is "similar to him" (*tadvad*), namely, like Cittavajra. Provoking [him] with "*Jinajik*," the mantra of emission, one should contemplate [him] in the centre of a moon-disc on a lotus[-seat] in the east.

The deity called Ratnadhṛk is
Ratneśa in the south, who resembles Kumāra with his faces.
The colour [of his body] is similar to blazing gold.
[He] holds an emerald and so forth in his [excellent] six hands. (v.75)

ānanaiḥ kumārābham (źal gźon nu 'dra) iti/ dakṣiṇavāmamadhyānanair nīlasitapītai[r] Mañjuśrī[92]sadṛśa[93][24b1]**taptatapanīyasaṃnibha** (btso ma'i gser gyi mdaṅs daṅ 'dra ba la) **marakataratnādiramyakaraṣaṭkam** (phyag drug ma rga da rin chen la sogs bsnams) iti/ bhāsvara[94]suvarṇṇasadṛśavarṇṇaṃ/ harita-maṇipadmakhaḍgacakraprajñāliṅganaiḥ/ śobhita[95]karaṣaṭkañ ca/ **Ratneśaṃ**[96] (rin chen 'byuṅ) [24b2]Ratnasaṃbhavaṃ ratnadhṛg iti saṃcodya Mañjuvajrasya **dakṣiṇato** (lho ru) dhyāyād iti sambandhaḥ/

ā ro lik[97] 'od dpag med pa dma ni/
rā ga ltar dmar źal gñis de daṅ 'dra/
'od zer 'bar źiṅ phyag na pa dma sogs/
mtshan ma bsnams pa nub tu bsam par bya//76//

ā ro lik ces pa dma rā ga bźin du dmar la źal gñis de bźin te/
snaṅ ba mtha' yas 'bar ba 'od ldan nub tu pad ma la sogs mtshan pa'i phyag//76//

---

92. Ms.: Mañjusrī.

93. Ms.: sadṛsa.

94. Ms.: bhāsura.

95. Ms.: sobhita.

96. Ms.: Ratnasa.

97. P.: ārolik ces.

"He resembles Kumāra with his faces (*kumārābha*)" means that he has the appearance of Mañjuśrī (i.e., Mañjuvajra) with his [three] faces, namely, right, left and central, which are blue, white and yellow [respectively], his complexion which is the colour of blazing gold (*taptatapanīyasaṃnibha<bhāsvarasuvarṇṇa-sadṛśavarṇṇa*) and his six hands beautified (*ramyakara-<śobhitakara-*) by the emerald and so forth, that is to say, [four beautified by holding] an emerald, a lotus, a sword, a wheel and [the remaining two by] embracing [his] consort. The sentence is completed as follows [supplying the subordinate and main verb]: arousing [him] with [the mantra] "*Ratnadhṛk*," one should contemplate Ratnasambhava (<Ratneśa) to the south of Mañjuvajra.

Ārolik is Amitābha, the one with flaring rays.
[Amitābha] is ruby-red and has two faces like his.
[His] hands are characterized by the lotus and the rest.
One should contemplate him in the west. (v. 76)

saroruharāgāruṇam (pa dma ni rā ga ltar dmar) iti/ padmarāgaval lohitam/ **ānanadvayan tadvad** (źal gñis de daṅ 'dra) iti kumā[24b3]rasyevāsyāpi dakṣiṇavāmavacane nīlasite[98] [/] **paṅkajādicihnakaram** (phyag na pa dma sogs mtshan ma bsnams pa) iti/ raktapadmakhaḍgacakramaṇiviśiṣṭa[99]karam iti/ Amitābham **ujjvalaprabham**[100] ('od zer 'bar źiṅ) āro[li]g iti saṃ[24b4]codya/ Mañjuvajrasya **paścimato dhyāyād** (nub tu bsam par bya) ityarthaḥ//

pra jñā dhṛk ces bya bas[101] don yod grub/
rin chen mar gad lta bu'i mdog ldan źiṅ/
sṅa ma lta bu'i źal sogs phun tshogs mṅa'[102]/
ral gri la sogs bsnams pa byaṅ du bsam//77//

ma ra ga ta'i nor bu lta bu'i sṅon bźin la sogs phun sum tshogs ldan pa/
byaṅ du don yod ces pa pra jñā dhrik ces ral gri la sogs rnam ldan pa//77//

98. Ms.: nīlasita.

99. Ms.: visiṣṭa.

100. Ms.: prabhām.

101. P. N.: daṅ.

102. P. N.: phun sum tshogs mṅa' ba.

[Amitābha is] ruby-red (*saroruharāgāruṇam<padmarāgavallohitam*). "[Amitābha's] two faces are like his" (*ānanadvayan tadvad*) because, like Kumāra (i.e., Mañjuśrī-Mañjuvajra), he has a blue face on the right and a white face on the left.

His hands are "characterized (*-cihna-*) by the lotus and the rest" means that [those of] his hands [that are not engaged in embracing his consort] are differentiated by [holding] a red lotus, a sword, a wheel and a jewel. It is implied (*ity arthaḥ*) that provoking Amitābha or "the one with flaring rays (*ujjvalaprabhā*)" with [the mantra] "*Ārolik*," [one] should contemplate him to the west of Mañjuvajra.

Prajñādhṛk, alias Amoghasiddhi, is emerald green in colour.
Beginning with faces, [he] has all the [characteristics] of the former
One characterized by a sword and the rest.
[One] should contemplate him in the north. (v. 77)

marakatamaṇiprakāśam[103] (rin chen mar gad lta bu'i mdog ldan źiṅ) iti haritaratnasadṛśavarṇṇam/ **prāg iva vadanādi sampadopetam** (sṅa ma lta bu'i źal sogs phun tshogs mṅa') iti/ nīlasita[24b5]dakṣiṇavāmamukhanānāvidha-kiraṇaspharaṇādisampattyā pūrva[vad] avanvitaṃ/ **kṛpāṇādyair** (ral gri la sogs) iti/ khaḍgacakrapadmaratnair **anvitaṃ** (bsnams pa)/ **Amoghasiddhi** (don yod grub) prajñādhṛg iti saṃcodya Mañju[25a1]vajrasy**ottara**[104]**to dhyāyād** (byaṅ du bsam) ityarthaḥ/

ral pa cod pan mdzes daṅ sna tshogs pa'i/
rin chen mchog gi 'od zer 'bar bas brgyan/
rig ma'i[105] mgon daṅ rab tu bcas pa'i sku/
thams cad ñi ma'i dkyil 'khor dag la bsam//78//

mdzes pa'i ral pa'i dbu rgyan sna tshogs rin chen 'od kyis rab brgyan pa/
rig ma daṅ bcas lus can thams cad ñi ma'i dkyil 'khor la ni bsam par bya//78//

103. Ms.: prakāsam.

104. Ms.: Mañjuvajrasyauttara.

105. P. N.: rig pa.

[Amoghasiddhi's] colour is emerald-green (*marakatamaṇiprakāśam<harita-ratnasadṛśavarṇam*). Beginning with faces, he has all [the characteristics] of the former (*prāg iva*), which is to say, that as before (*pūrvavat*) he has blue and white faces on the right and left and is bright with multi-coloured rays.

"With a sword and the rest" means that he is holding a sword, a wheel, a lotus and a jewel. [As before,] it is implied that one should provoke Amoghasiddhi with [the mantra] "*Prajñādhṛk*," and [one] should contemplate him to the north of Mañjuvajra.

[The five Buddhas] have shining matted locks
Which are brilliantly adorned with various precious jewels.
[The Buddhas] whose bodies are embraced by consorts
Should be contemplated all on the sun-discs. (v. 78)

sarveṣām eva samānāni viśeṣaṇāny[106] āha[107]/ ruciretyādi/ **rucirajaṭāmukuṭāś**[108] (ral pa cod pan mdzes) ca te **uttamanānāprabhābhir** (sna tshogs pa'i rin chen mchog gi) **ujjvalābharaṇāś**[109] **ce**('od zer 'bar bas brgyan)ti tathoktam/[25a2] **vidyāsanāthavapuṣa** (rig ma'i mgon daṅ rab tu bcas pa'i sku) iti āliṅgita-svābhaprajñāḥ **sarva** (thams cad) iti Vairocanād anye ravimaṇḍale dhyeyāḥ/ Vairocanasya candrāsaneno[110]ktatvāt/

mo ha ra ti źes pas lha mo spyan/
zla ba'i[111] dkyil 'khor rdzogs pa la gnas pa/
mchog tu sgeg[112] ciṅ sku yi rdo rje 'dra/
me yi phyogs ñid du ni bsam par bya//79//

me yi phyogs mtshams su ni mo ha ra ti źes pas lha mo spyan mar gyur/
bzlas pa rdzogs pa'i dkyil 'khor la gnas mchog gi 'jo sgeg sku yi rdo rje'i mdog//79//

---

106. Ms.: viseṣeṇāny.

107. Ms.: *ha* inserted from margin.

108. Ms.: mukuṭās.

109. Ms.: ujjvalābharaṇās.

110. *candrāsanena* is ungrammatical. It may be a corruption of *candrāsanatvena*.

111. P. N.: zla ba.

112. P. N.: sreg.

In the verse beginning with "shining (*rucira*)," [he] explains the features common to all [the five Buddhas]. He says that they have shining diadems on their piled-up matted locks (*rucirajaṭāmukuṭāḥ* = *rucirā mukuṭā yeṣāṃ jaṭāsu te...*), ornaments that shine with the fine and many-coloured radiances [of jewels] (*uttamanānāprabhābhir*), and bodies accompanied by [their] Wisdoms (*vidyā-*), that is to say, embraced by consorts [emanated] in their likeness. When he says that all [the Buddhas] should be contemplated (i.e., seated) on sun-discs he means all except Vairocana (*Vairocanād anye*), for it has already been explained [in verse 74] that Vairocana has a moon-disc as his seat.

With the mantra "*Moharati*,"
Arousing the supreme goddess Locanā sitting on a full moon-disc,
One should meditate on her as erotic and like Kāyavajra
In the fire direction (i.e., southeast). (v. 79)

sṛṅgāra[113]**kāyavajrābhe**(sgeg ciṅ sku yi rdo rje 'dra)ti/ śṛṅgā[25a3]ra[114] rasānvitaṃ mukhādibhi[r] Vairocanasadṛśī **pūrṇṇacandrasthā** (zla ba'i dkyil 'khor rdzogs pa la gnas pa) **parame**(mchog tu)ti viśuddharūpā[115] **Locanādevī** (lha mo spyan) moharatīti mantreṇa saṃcodanād[116] **āgneye dikpradeśe**[117] (me yi phyogs ñid du ni) syāt/ dhyānena tatra[25a4]draṣṭavyety arthaḥ/

dve ṣa ra ti[118] źes pa dga' ba che/
dga' chen mchog 'dod mā ma kī źes pa/
źal mdzes phyag rnams thugs kyi gtso 'dra ba/
rnam par sgeg pa bden bral mtshams su bsam//80//

bden bral dag la sgeg mo thugs kyi dbaṅ phyug lta bur mdzes pa'i źal/
dve ṣa ra ti źes pas dga' ba mchog tu spro ba mā ma kī źes bya//80//

nairṛtī(bden bral mtshams su)tyādi/ **mahārataparamotsukā** (dga' chen mchog 'dod) Māmakī yathoktarūpā dveṣaratīti saṃcoditā nairṛtikoṇe draṣṭavyety arthaḥ/

---

113. Ms.: sṛṅgāra.

114. Ms.: sṛṅgāra.

115. Ms.: visuddharūpā.

116. Ms.: saṃcodyanād.

117. Ms.: dikpradese.

118. D. C.: dve ṣa ra tī.

[Verse 79] By saying that she is erotic and like Kāyavajra (*śṛṅgāra-kāyavajrābhā*), he means that she embodies the sentiment of love (*śṛṅgāra-rasaḥ*) and resembles Vairocana in her faces and other [features]. Seated on a full moon-disc and supreme, that is to say, pure of form, the goddess Locanā should be in the southeast direction after having been aroused with the mantra "*Moharati*." It is implied that one should see her there by means of visualization.

Arousing Māmakī with the mantra "*Dveṣarati*,"
The one who intensely desires the supreme act of love,
One should meditate on the coquettish [goddess] in Nairṛti's corner (i.e., southwest).
[Her] beautiful faces and arms are similar to Citteśa's. (v. 80)

[He explains the verse] beginning with the words "in Nairṛti's (southwest) corner." Māmakī, who intensely desires the supreme act of love (*mahārata-paramotsukā*), should be aroused with the mantra "*Dveṣarati*" and then visualized in the southwest corner in the form indicated [in this verse].

rā ga ra ti źes bya yum mchog ni/
gos dkar yon tan rin chen mtha' yas pa/
dri med sku ni gsuṅ gi dbaṅ phyug 'dra/
rluṅ gi phyogs su rnam par bsam par bya//81//

ṅag dbaṅ dri med sku ni rā ga ra ti źes bya yum mchog ni/
mchog gi rjes su dkar mo źes par mtha' yas yon tan rin chen ma//81//

vāgīśāmala[119]**dehe**(dri med sku ni gsuṅ gi dbaṅ phyug 'dra)ti Amitābha[25a5] van nirmalavarṇṇādiśarīrā[120] **Pāṇḍarākhyā**[121] (gos dkar) {yathārūpā} yathoktarūpā **rāgaratīti** (rā ga ra ti źes bya){/} saṃcoditā **prabhañjanāśāyā[ṃ]**[122](rluṅ gi phyogs su) draṣṭavyā/

va jra ra tis[123] rab bskul sgrol ma ni/
dri med rin chen 'od kyi phreṅ ba yis/
phyogs kyi tshogs khebs raṅ gi ṅo bo ni/
rin chen dbaṅ 'dra dbaṅ ldan phyogs su bsam//82//

rin chen dbaṅ phyug [']dra ba'i dṅos po sgrol ba ba dzra ra ti źes bskul bas/ dri med rin chen phreṅ bas bsgoms pa'i phyogs 'khor byed ma dbaṅ ldan la//82//

---

119. Ms.: vāgīsāmala.

120. Ms.: sarīrā.

121. Ms.: Paṇḍarākhyā.

122. Ms.: prabhañjanāsāyā.

123. D. C.: tīs.

Provoking Paṇḍarā with the mantra "*Rāgarati*,"
The supreme queen who has infinite merits and jewels,
[Her] stainless body similar to the King of speech,
One should meditate on her in the wind corner (i.e., northwest). (v. 81)

Verse 81 (*vāgīśāmaladeheti*). [Her] stainless body is similar to that of "the King of speech (*Vāgīśa*)," in other words, her pure body shows a resemblance to Amitābha in colour and so forth. Provoking her with the mantra "*Rāgarati*," one should visualize the goddess named Paṇḍarā in the northwest direction in the form given [here] (*yathārūpā<yathoktarūpā*).

Arousing Tārā with the mantra "*Vajrarati*,"
Who covers all directions with a bundle of rays of stainless jewels,
One should meditate on her in Ratneśa's likeness
In Īśāna's corner (i.e., northeast). (v. 82)

Ratneśavat[124] (rin chen dbaṅ 'dra) surūpa{ṇṇa}va[r]ṇṇādibhī Ratnasambhava-sadṛ[k][25a6] **Tārā** (sgrol ma) yatho[kta]viśeṣaṇā[125]/ vajraratīti **pracoditā** (rab bskul)/ **aiśāne**[126] **dikpradeśe**[127] (dbaṅ ldan phyogs su) draṣṭavyā/

lha mo 'di rnams ṅes pa'i phyag mtshan ni/
'khor lo bzaṅ daṅ u tpal dmar po daṅ/
pa dma u tpal gser mdog rim bźin bsam/
lhag ma rnams ni bdag po ji bźin 'dod//83//

dam pa'i 'khor lo u tpal dmar po pa dma u tpal ser po rnams kyis mtshan/
de dag gi ni rim pa'i ṅes pa'i lhag ma'i ji ltar 'dod pa'i phyag bsnams yin//83//

āsāṃ pradhānacihnāny āha// **saccakre**('khor lo bzaṅ)tyādi/ **śiṣṭhānī**(lhag ma rnams ni)ti[128] Locanāyāḥ/ khadgapadma[25b1]maṇayaḥ/ pariśiṣṭāni[129] cihnāni evaṃ Māmakyāḥ/ Pāṇḍarāyā[ḥ][130] khadgacakramaṇayaḥ/ Tārāyāḥ khaḍgapadma-maṇaya ityarthaḥ/

---

124. Ms.: Ratneṣavan.

125. Ms.: viseṣaṇā.

126. Ms.: aisāne.

127. Ms.: dikpradese.

128. Ms.: siṣṭhānīti.

129. Ms.: parisiṣṭāni.

130. Ms.: Paṇḍarāyā.

Like Ratneśa, resembling Ratnasambhava in such features as her form (*svarūpa*) and colour, Tārā, with the characteristics stated (*yatho[kta]viśeṣaṇā*), should be aroused with the mantra "*Vajrarati*" and visualized in the northeast corner.

The obligatory symbols of these goddesses are
Excellent wheel, red water lily (*utpala*),
Lotus and golden water lily, respectively.
The other [symbols] are at one's choice. (v. 83)

In the verse beginning with the words "excellent wheel (*saccakra*)," he explains the principal symbols of those [goddesses]. The remaining symbols[, held in their other hands,] are, for Locanā, sword, lotus and jewel; for Māmakī, the same; for Pāṇḍarā, sword, wheel and jewel; and for Tārā, sword, lotus and jewel.

de ñid gsum gyis gzugs kyi rdo rje sogs/
lha mo[131] rnams ni sku la sogs 'dra bar/
dkyil 'khor gyi ni mtshams gyur bźi po daṅ/
rtsa ba'i sgo yi ṅos gñis dag tu bsam//84//

dkyil 'khor grva bźi daṅ ni śar gyi sgo gñis la ni bsam bya ba/
gzugs sogs rdo rje lha mo sku la sogs daṅ gsum gyis so//84//

maṇḍale(dkyil 'khor gyi ni)tyādi/ āgneyādiṣu **caturṣu koṇeṣu** (mtshams gyur bźi po daṅ) **mūladvārapārśvadvaye**[132] (rtsa ba'i sgo yi ṅos gñis dag tu) ca **Rūpa**[25b2]**vajrādayaḥ** (gzugs kyi rdo rje sogs){/} ṣaṭ **devyo** (lha mo rnams ni) yathākramaṃ **kāyavajrādinibhā** (sku la sogs 'dra bar) **tatv[atray]ene**(de ñid gsum gyis)ti{/} Oṃ Āḥ Hūṃ iti mantreṇotsṛjya[133] yathāvidhi vakṣamāṇa-darppaṇādipradhānacihnā **dhyātavyā** (bsam)/ ityarthaḥ/ tatra kāyo[134] Vairo[25b3]canas tatsadṛśī[135] darppaṇacihnā/ khaḍga[padma]maṇipariśiṣṭacihnā[136] ca Rūpavajrā/

131. N.: mos.

132. Ms.: mūladvārapārsvadvaye.

133. Ms.: mantreṇotsṛja.

134. Ms.: kāye.

135. Ms.: tansadṛśī.

136. Ms.: parisiṣṭacihnā.

With three truths, one should contemplate
The goddesses beginning with Rūpavajrā,
In the likeness of Kāya and others [respectively],
In the four corners and on both sides of the main gate [of the maṇḍala]. (v. 84)

Verse 84 (*maṇḍaletyādi*). "With [three] realities," that is to say, with the mantra "*Oṃ Āḥ Hūṃ*," he should send forth the six goddesses beginning with Rūpavajrā, [visualizing them] in the likeness of the [six Tathāgatas] beginning with Kāyavajra, to the four corners beginning with that in the southeast and to either side of the main gate [of the maṇḍala]. Then, in accordance with the prescribed rule (*yathāvidhi*), he should visualize them holding the mirror and other principal symbols that will be stated below. Of these [six pairs] (*tatra*), Kāya (i.e., Kāyavajra) is Vairocana and [the goddess] in his likeness is Rūpavajrā, holding a mirror as [her principal] symbol and a sword[, a lotus] and a jewel as her remaining symbols.

Śabdavajrā[137] Cittavajranibhā vīṇācihnā khaḍgapadmamaṇipariśiṣṭacihnā[138] ca/ Gandhavajrā Ratneśa[139]nibhā gandha[25b4]śaṃkhacihnā[140]/ khaḍgapadmacakra-pariśiṣṭacihnā[141] ca/ Rasavajrā Vāgvajranibhā svādurasādhārapūrṇṇa-padmabhāṇḍacihnā/ khaḍgacakramaṇipariśiṣṭacihnā[142] ca/ Sparśavajrā Amoghasi [25b5]ddhinibhā vastracihnā/ khaḍgapadmamaṇipariśiṣṭacihnā[143] ca/ Dharmadhātuvajrā Vajrasatvanibhā dharmodayamudrācihnā/ khaḍgapadma-maṇipariśiṣṭacihnā[144] ca/ pūrṇṇendumaṇḍalastheti/[25b6]ca pūr{ṇṇa}rvvam uktaṃ/ sarvāsu devīsu yojya[ṃ]/

ya mā nta kṛt[145] ces byas gśin rje gśed/
mtha' yas 'jigs 'od phyogs kun khyab daṅ ldan/
dus mtha' mi bzad sprin gyi dkyil 'khor mdog/
thugs kyi rgyal po dag daṅ sku mtshuṅs pa//85//

śar gyi sgo ru grags pa bsam pa thams cad 'grub mtha' yas pas 'jigs pa'i 'od/
'bar la ya ma nta krit ces pas zad dus drag sprin dkyil 'khor dṅos po ste//85//

---

137. Ms.: Sabdavajrā.

138. Ms.: parisiṣṭacihnā.

139. Ms.: Ratnesa.

140. Ms.: gandhasaṃkhacihnā.

141. Ms.: parisiṣṭacihnā.

142. Ms.: parisiṣṭacihnā.

143. Ms.: parisiṣṭacihnā.

144. Ms.: parisiṣṭacihnā.

145. N.: krit.

In the likeness of Cittavajra is Śabdavajrā, holding a lute as [her principal] symbol and a sword, a lotus and a jewel as her remaining symbols. In the likeness of Ratneśa is Gandhavajrā, holding a perfume[-filled] conch shell (*gandhaśaṅkha*) as [her principal] symbol and a sword, a lotus and a wheel as her remaining symbols. In the likeness of Vāgvajra is Rasavajrā, holding a skull-cup full of sweet-juiced [fruits] (*svādurasādhārapūrṇṇapadmabhāṇḍa*) as [her principal] symbol and a sword, a wheel and a jewel as her remaining symbols. In the likeness of Amoghasiddhi is Sparśavajrā, holding a garment (*vastra*) as [her principal] symbol and a sword, a lotus and a jewel as her remaining symbols. In the likeness of Vajrasattva is Dharmadhātuvajrā, holding a *dharmodaya* [triangle] as [her principal] symbol and a sword, a lotus and a jewel as her remaining symbols. It has been already explained that [Locanā] is [seated] on a full-moon disc. This adjective should be understood here to apply to each of the [six] goddesses.

[One should contemplate] Yamāntakṛt, alias Yamāntaka, in the likeness of
Cittādhirāja.
His complexion resembles the dense threatening clouds
That will appear at the end of an aeon,
And his infinite and terrible rays fill all the directions. (v. 85)

idānīṃ dvārapālakrodhān āha/ **pūrvadvāra** (śar gyi sgo na) ityādi/ sarvāśā[146]-varttin yo anantābhīmā ābhā asyeti **sarvāśā**[147]**vartyanantabhīmābhaḥ**[148] (mtha' yas 'jigs 'od phyogs kun khyab daṅ ldan)//[26a1]**kṣayograghanamaṇḍala cchāya** (dus mtha' mi bzad sprin gyi dkyil 'khor mdog) iti pralaya-kālogrameghasamūhākāraḥ/ **Cittādhirājo** (thugs kyi rgyal po) Akṣobhyas tena **samā** (mtshuṅs pa) bhujamukhādibhis tulyā yā **tanur** (sku) Yamāriśarīraḥ[149]//

drag po'i rigs 'od dpag med rnam 'phro bas/
gśin rje mthar mdzad śin tu gdug pa yi/
sbrul gyis lus kyi yan lag rnam brgyan pa/
dpal ldan śar gyi sgo na[150] bsam par bya//86//

thugs bdag rgyal po mñam pa'i sku ni du ma'i khro bo rigs kyi 'od phyuṅ ba/ gśin rje mthar byed ces bya mi bzad[151] pa yi sbrul gyis sku brgyan dpal ldan pa'o//86//

---

146. Ms.: sarvāsā.

147. Ms.: sarvāsa.

148. Ms.: bhīmābhaṃ.

149. Ms.: Yamārisarīraḥ.

150. D. C.: sgo ni.

151. P. N.: zad.

Now, in the verse beginning with the words "in the eastern gate," he speaks of the wrathful gatekeepers. [The gatekeeper of the east] is described as "one whose infinite and terrible rays fill all the directions [of space] (*sarvāśāvartyanantabhīmābhaṃ<sarvāśāvartin yo anantā bhīmā ābhā asya*)," and as one whose complexion resembles the dense threatening clouds that will appear at the end of the aeon (*kṣayograghanamaṇḍalacchāya<pralayakālogrameghasamūhākāraḥ*). He looks like Cittādhirāja, that is to say, Yamāri's body shows a resemblance to Akṣobhya's in the arms, faces and so forth.

He is the exterminator of Death (*Vaivasvatāntakārin*)
Who emits plenty of rays of clans of wrathful [deities],
And his limbs are adorned with ferocious snakes.
One should meditate on the possessor of wealth at the eastern gate. (v. 86)

tato vini[ḥ]sṛtānām[152] **anekā**[26a2]**raudra**[153]**kulānāṃ bhābhir** (drag po'i rigs 'od dpag med) upalakṣitaḥ/ krūrā bhujaṅgā[154] aṅgabhūṣaṇam asyeti **krūra-bhujaṅgāṅgai[r] bhūṣaṇaḥ** (śin tu gdug pa yi sbrul gyis lus kyi yan lag rnam brgyan pa)/ **śrīmān**[155] (dpal ldan) sarvārthasampannaḥ/ sa evaṃbhūto **vaivasvantāntakārī**(gśin rje mthar mdzad)ti Yamāntako yamāntakṛd ity e[26a3]vaṃ saṃcoditaḥ san[156] bhāsvatīti sūryamaṇḍale pūrvadvārasthakhyātaṃ prasthitaḥ/ tatra draṣṭavya iti yāvat/

pra jñā nta kṛt[157] ces byas bla med 'od/
drag ciṅ phyag sogs sku yi rdo rje 'dra/
gźan gyis mi thub ces bya gtum po ni/
lho phyogs kyi ni sgo ru bsam par bya//87//

lho phyogs kyi sgor gnas pa pra dzñā nta krit ces pas bla na med ldan pa/
sku yi dbaṅ phyug bźin du phyag la sogs pa drag po gźan gyis mi thub gsal//87//

152. Ms.: dhinisṛtānām.

153. Ms.: rodra.

154. Ms.: krūrāṃbhujaṅga.

155. Ms.: srīmān.

156. Ms.: sata.

157. N.: krit.

[He] is revealed (*upalakṣitaḥ*) by the rays of many (*aneka-*) clans of wrathful [deities] that have come forth from that [body of his], his limbs are adorned with the ferocious Snake[-deities] (*krūrā bhujaṅgā aṅgabhūṣaṇam asyeti krūrabhujaṅgāṅgair bhūṣaṇaḥ*), [and] he is the possessor of wealth (*śrīmān*) in the sense that he is richly endowed (*sampannaḥ*) with all that is beneficial (*sarvārtha-*). Once this (*evaṃbhūtaḥ*) exterminator of Death (*vaivasvatāntakārī <yamāntaka*) has been aroused (*saṃcoditaḥ san*) with [the mantra] "*Yamāntakṛt*," he is said to be at the eastern gate [of the maṇḍala], that is to say, he should be visualized standing before it on a sun-disc (*bhāsvati< sūryamaṇḍale*).

With [the mantra] "*Prajñāntakṛt*,"
[Provoking] the ferocious one, the supreme light, in the likeness of Kāyeśa,
The furious [deity] named the invincible (Aparājita),
One should meditate on [him] at the southern gate. (v. 87)

dakṣiṇetyādi/ jagadandhakārāpahāritvād **anuttarajyotiḥ** (bla med 'od)/ **kāyeśo**[158] (sku yi rdo rje) Vairocana[26a4]s tadvadbhujamukhavarṇṇair **ugraḥ** (drag ciṅ)/ sa evambhūtaḥ/ kleśādi[159]mārair anabhibhūtatvād **Aparājitaḥ** (gźan gyis mi thub)/ **prasahaḥ** (gtum po ni) pracaṇḍarūpaḥ **prajñāntakṛd ity** (pra jñā nta kṛt ces) evaṃ saṃcoditaḥ san[160]/ **dakṣiṇadigdvārastho** (lho phyogs kyi ni sgo ru) bhāsvati **dra**[26a5]**ṣṭavyaḥ** (bsam par bya)/

pad mā nta krit[161] ces byas phyogs rnams kyi[162]/
'khor lo'i[163] 'od kyis mṅon par khebs byed pa/
'od mdaṅs 'jig[164] dus me 'drar 'jigs par ldan/
phyag la sogs par gsuṅ gi rdo rje 'dra//88//

de nas rta mgrin nub kyi phyogs kyi sgo ru 'od zer 'khrigs pas phyogs bskor ba/
pa dmā nta kṛt ces pas 'bar ba'i 'jig[165] pa'i me ltar 'jigs pa'i gzugs//88//

---

158. Ms.: kāyeso.

159. Ms.: klesādi.

160. Inserted from margin.

161. P.: pa dma nta kṛt; N.: pa dma nta krit.

162. P. N.: kyis.

163. P. N.: los.

164. P. N.: 'jigs.

165. P. N.: 'jigs.

Verse 87 (*dakṣiṇetyādi*). The supreme light (*anuttarajyotiḥ*), [so called] because he removes the darkness of the world, in the likeness of Kāyeśa[, that is to say, like] Vairocana in his arms, faces and complexion, [but] ferocious (*ugraḥ*), named "the invincible" (*Aparājitaḥ*) because he was not overcome by Defilement (*kleśaḥ*) or any other of the Māras, and furious (*prasahaḥ*< *pracaṇḍarūpaḥ*), he should [first] be aroused with [the mantra] "*Prajñāntakṛt*" and visualized on a sun[-disc] at the southern gate.

With [the mantra] "*Padmāntakṛt*,"
[Provoking the wrathful deity] whose halo covers all the directions,
Whose complexion is like the fire that will flare up at the end of the aeon,
He resembles Vāgvajra in [his characteristics] beginning with arms. (v. 88)

gdug pa du ma rnam gnon 'jigs pa'i źal/
thub dbaṅ ha ha źes ni bźad pa yis/
ri bor bcas pa sgyel bas skrag mdzad pa/
rta mgrin de bźin nub kyi phyogs su bsam//89//

gsuṅ gi bźin du phyag la sogs pa du mas sdaṅ ba 'jigs byed źal/
gad sgrogs bźad pas ri rnams g-yo bar byed daṅ thub pa'i dbaṅ rnams so//89//

hayakandharetyādi[166] **Vāgvajravadbhujādyair** (phyag la sogs par gsuṅ gi rdo rje 'dra) iti bhujamukhavarṇṇair Amitābhasadṛśaḥ/ yathoktapariśeṣaṇo[167] Hayagrīvaḥ/ padmāntakṛd ity evaṃ saṃcoditaḥ{/} san paścimadvā[26b1]re bhāsvanmaṇḍale[168] draṣṭavya iti saṃkṣepārthaḥ/

vi ghnān ta kṛt ces byas dpa' bo ni/
dus mtha'i me ltar drag po bdud rtsi 'khyil/
'phags pa'i źal[169] sogs mi bskyod daṅ mtshuṅs pa/
de bźin byaṅ gi sgo ru bsam par bya//90//

de nas mi bskyod 'dra ba'i źal sogs vi ghna nta krit ces bya byaṅ sgo ru/
zad dus byin za lta bu 'phags pa bdud rtsi 'khyil ba dpa' ba'o//90//

---

166. Ms.: hayakandaretyādi.

167. Ms.: pariseṣaṇo.

168. Ms.: bhāsvanmaṇḍala.

169. Ms.: P. N.: źabs.

With his fearful face,
The King of ascetics (*munīndra*) haw-haws so loudly that it upsets the mountain
And terrifies plenty of vicious people.
One should meditate on such Hayagrīva at the western gate. (v. 89)

Verses 88 and 89 (*hayakandharetyādi*). Resembling Vāgvajra in [his] arms and other [characteristics], that is to say, resembling Amitābha in his arms, faces and complexion, Hayagrīva, who has the [additional] characteristics stated [in this passage] (*yathoktaviśeṣaṇo* [em.]), should be aroused with the mantra "*Padmāntakṛt*" and visualized on a sun-disc at the western gate. This in brief is the meaning of the verses.

With [the mantra] "*Vighnāntakṛt*," [provoking] the hero, noble Amṛtakuṇḍalin,
Resembling Akṣobhya in his faces and so forth,
And fearsome as the fire that will flare up at the end of the aeon,
One should meditate on such [a deity] at the northern gate. (v. 90)

Vighnāntakotsargam āha/ **Akṣobhyavad** (mi bskyod daṅ mtshuṅs pa) ityādi/ bhujamukhavarṇṇair Akṣobhyasadṛśaḥ/ **pralayakālānalavad ugra** (dus mtha'i me ltar drag po) āryo [']**mṛtakuṇḍalin**[170] (bdud rtsi 'khyil) / pā[26b2]pair yo dharmebhya ārā{ryā}ta[171]tvād **āryaḥ** ('phags pa)/ sakalavighnavināśatvād[172] **vīraḥ** (dpa' bo)/ **vighnāntakṛd ity** (vi ghnān ta kṛt ces byas) evaṃ saṃcoditaḥ {/} sann **uttaradvāre** (byaṅ gi sgo ru) sūryamaṇḍalastho **dhyeya** (bsam par bya) ity arthaḥ/

rnam par snaṅ mdzad thugs gtso 'od dpag med/
thugs kyi dbaṅ po rim bźin cod pan yin/
tho ba dbyug pa de bźin pad ma daṅ/
rdo rje sogs 'di phyag ni kun la bsam//91//

rnam snaṅ mdzad daṅ thub dbaṅ snaṅ ba mtha' yas thugs kyi dbaṅ phyug dbu rgyan daṅ/
rim par tho[173] ba be con pa dma rdo rje la sogs phyag kyaṅ de bźin no//91//

170. Ms.: āryomṛtakuṇḍaliḥ.

171. Ms.: Thagana's commentary: 'phags pa źes bya ba ni sdig pa mi dge ba'i chos rnams las riṅ du gyur pa'o//

172. Ms.: sakalavighnavināsatvād.

173. N.: mtho.

In the next verse, beginning with the words "Resembling Akṣobhya," he speaks of the emission of Vighnāntaka. Resembling Akṣobhya in his arms, faces and complexion [but] fearsome as the fire that will flare up at the end of the aeon (*pralayakālānalavad ugraḥ*), the noble (*āryo*) Amṛtakuṇḍalin, noble because he is far from the sinful *dharma*s, a hero (*vīraḥ*) because he removes all obstacles, should be aroused with [the mantra] "*Vighnāntakṛt*" and visualized on a sun-disc at the northern gate.

[There are] Vairocana, Citteśa (or Munīndra), Amitābha and Citteśa
On their crowns respectively.
In all their hands, one should visualize
A hammer, staff, lotus, thunderbolt and so forth. (v. 91)

Vairocanetyādi/ e[26b3]ṣām eva Yamāryādīnām abhiṣekānantaraṃ makuṭeṣu kramaśo[174] Vairocanākṣobhyāmitābhāmoghasiddhi draṣṭavyāḥ// mudgarādīni catvāri pradhānacihnāni yathākramaṃ kare dhyātavyāni/[26b4]ādiśabdāt khaḍgādīny[175] api yathāyogaṃ yojyānīty arthaḥ[/] krodharūpatve 'pi kṛpālūnāṃ satvavinayam eva[176] prayojanaṃ/ tad uktam{/} mahāsamayatatve/ aho hi sarvabuddhānāṃ vajrakarmama[26b5]hādṛḍham/ yacchāntā raudratā[ṃ] yāṃti raudrāṇāṃ hitahetuneti/ tathā guhyatilake aho hi vaśitājñānaṃ[177] buddhānāṃ tattvadarśināṃ tatra hy upāyavinayāḥ krodhatvaṃ yānti nirmmalā i[27a1]tyādi/

---

174. Ms.: kramaso.

175. Ms.: ādisabdārn khaḍgādīny.

176. Ms.: satvaviyanamaiva.

177. Ms.: vasitājñānaṃ.

Verse 91 (*Vairocanetyādi*). Immediately after empowering these [wrathful gatekeepers] beginning with Yamāri (i.e., Yamāntaka), one should visualize on their crowns Vairocana, Akṣobhya, Amitābha and Amoghasiddhi respectively.[178] One should meditate on the four principal symbols beginning with the hammer [by visualizing one of them] in [the main right] hand of [one after another of the four gatekeepers] in accordance with the order [stated in this verse]. The word "and so forth" (*ādi*) indicates that one should assign [the other symbols] beginning with a sword to their [remaining] hands, as is customary (*yathā-yogaṃ*). Although they are wrathful in appearance, they are compassionate, and their only purpose [in assuming this appearance] is to train sentient beings. This has been explained in the *Mahāsamayatattva*:[179] "Indeed the adamantine action of all the Buddhas is supremely sure, for (*yat*), [though] serene (*śāntāḥ*), they become violent (*raudratāṃ yānti*) for the benefit (*hitahetunā*) of the violent." The same [is taught] in the *Guhyatilaka* in the passage that begins "How wonderful the wisdom by which the enlightened (*tattvadarśinām*) Buddhas subjugate [others]. For in that [wisdom, although they are] free of contamination [by the *kleśa*s], they become wrathful, training [sentient beings] in accordance with expediency (*upāyavinayāḥ*)."

---

178. According to the verse and other commentaries, the deity meditated on Vighnāntaka's crown should be not Amoghasiddhi but Citteśa or Akṣobhya.

179. The *Mahāsamayatattva* corresponds to the 13th tantra of the Vajraśekhara cycle. However, this verse is not found in the *Mimi sanmei dajiaowang jing* 祕密三昧大教王經 (Taisho 883), which Sakai identified as the 13th tantra of the *Vajraśekhara*.

de ltar yoṅs su rdzogs pa'i dkyil 'khor la/
dṅos po thams cad kyis ni bltas nas kyaṅ/
sñiṅ po'i sṅags kyi 'od zer lcags kyu yis/
draṅs nas bde bar gśegs rnams bsgom par bya//92//

de ltar rdzogs par bskyed par dkyil 'khor mthoṅ nas dṅos po thams cad kyis/
sṅags kyi 'od zer lcags kyus bde gśegs spyan draṅs bsgom par bya//92//

iti parita[180] ityādi/ ity anantaroktena krameṇa paritaḥ{/} sarvathā **niṣpannamaṇḍalaṃ** (rdzogs pa'i dkyil 'khor la) **sarvabhāvenā**[181]**valokya** (dṅos po thams cad kyis ni bltas nas kyaṅ){/} jñānasatva**hṛnmantrasya** (sñiṅ po'i sṅags kyi) **mayūkhā** evā**ṃkuśās**[182] ('od zer lcags kyu yis) taiḥ **samāhṛtān** (draṅs nas) ākṛ[27a2]ṣṭān **sugatān** (bde bar gśegs rnams) maṇḍalacakrākārān samayamaṇḍalapurovarttino **bhāvayet** (bsgom par bya)/ etena jñānamaṇḍalākarṣaṇam uktam/

180. Ms.: iti paraita.

181. Ms.: sarvabhāvanā.

182. Ms.: evāṃkusās.

In this way, once having seen
The completed maṇḍala with intense devotion,
Drawing [them] down with the ray-hook of the heart-mantra,
One should meditate on Sugatas. (v. 92)

Verse 92 (*iti parita ityādi*). In accordance with the sequence just mentioned (*iti<anantaroktena krameṇa*), he should visualize with intense devotion the fully completed maṇḍala, and drawing down the Buddhas with the hook[-like] rays (*mayūkhā evāṅkuśās*) of the Knowledge being's heart-mantra he should visualize [them] in front of the Pledge-maṇḍala in the arrangement of the maṇḍala assembly. In this passage, he has explained how one is to draw down the Knowledge-maṇḍala.

śes rab thabs kyi raṅ bźin dri med pa'i/
tiṅ 'dzin las byuṅ dam pa'i bdes gaṅ bar/
'khor lo bsams nas de nas gśin rje ni/
mthar byed la sogs bśad pas bsruṅ bar bya//93//

thabs daṅ śes rab dṅos po dri med tiṅ 'dzin las byuṅ dam pa'i bde bas gsaṅ bar ni/
dkyil 'khor bsams te de nas mthar byed la sogs bsruṅ byas nas//93//

prajñety ādi/ prajñā strīrūpa ākāraḥ upāyaḥ puruṣarūpaḥ prajño [27a3]pāyamayaḥ **prajñopāyasvabhāvo** (śes rab thabs kyi raṅ bźin) yo [']yam amalaḥ **samādhis** (tiṅ 'dzin las) tataḥ **sambhūtaṃ** (byuṅ) yat **satsukhaṃ** (dam pa'i bdes) ten**āpūrṇṇaṃ** (gaṅ bar) tac **cakram** ('khor lo)/ **antaka** (mthar byed) mathan**ādyair** (la sogs) iti Yamāntakādibhiḥ{/} **kṛtārakṣaḥ**[183] (bsruṅ bar bya) san [27a4]yogī dhyāyāt/ etac ca samayamaṇḍale [']pi draṣṭavya[ṃ]/

---

183. Ms.: kṛtārakṣaḥ.

Filled up with the supreme pleasure
Arisen from the stainless meditation whose nature is wisdom and means,
One should visualize the troop [of the deities]
And make Yamāntaka and others protect [it]. (v. 93)

Verse 93 (*prajñety ādi*). The yogi should protect [the assembly] with Yamāntaka and the other (*yamāntakādibhiḥ/antakamathanādyaiḥ*) [wrathful deities] and meditate on the assembly (*cakra*) as being completely filled (*āpūrṇṇam*) with the supreme pleasure that arises from the stainless trance whose nature is both Wisdom and Means (*prajñopāyasvabhāvo<prajñopāya-mayaḥ*). Wisdom [here] is the female (*strīrūpaḥ*) aspect (*ākāraḥ*) and Means the masculine. One should perform the same meditation on the Pledge-maṇḍala.

The Procedures for Maṇḍala Offerings (Sanskrit Commentary)

raṅ gi sñiṅ pos mṅon bzlas mchod yon ni/
tsan dan bzaṅ sogs me tog gis mdzes dbul/
raṅ las byas pa lta bur dbaṅ bskur źiṅ/
cho ga yis ni mṅon par mchod par bya//94//

raṅ sñiṅ bzlas pa'i [dam pa'i][184] tsan dan sogs daṅ me tog mdzes pa phul te thim/
raṅ daṅ 'dra ba'i cho gas dbaṅ bskur byas nas 'di ltar nan tan mchod par bya//94//

svahṛdeti svabījen**ābhijaptaṃ** (raṅ gi sñiṅ pos mṅon bzlas) **saccandanā-dikusumāḍyam** (tsan dan bzaṅ sogs me tog gis mdzes) **arghan** (mchod yon) tasmai maṇḍalacakrāya **datvā** (dbul) tan maṇḍa[la]cakran yathāsvaṃ Yamā[27a5]ntakādikṛtākarṣaṇapraveśana[185]bandhanatoṣaṇakrameṇa samayamaṇḍale sikatāsv iva tailam antarbhāvya tad evaṃ {sa}pariniṣpanna[ṃ] maṇḍalacakra[ṃ] **svam ivāhitābhiṣeka**[27a6]**m** (raṅ las byas pa lta bur dbaṅ bskur źiṅ) iti Mañjuvajram iva{/} sevādikrameṇa kṛtābhiṣeka[ṃ] iti vakṣyamāṇena **vidhinā** (cho ga yis ni)/ prayataḥ sann **abhyarccayet** (mṅon par mchod par bya) pūjayet/ tatra yo maṇḍaladevatānāṃ niṣpattikra[27b1]maḥ/ sā sāmānyasevā 'dhimātra-niṣyandanaphalā/

184. D. C. have a lacuna here.

185. Ms.: pravesana.

The Procedures for Maṇḍala Offerings (English Translation)

Presenting oblations abounding in flowers, excellent sandalwood and so forth,
Consecrated by the muttered recitation of each heart[-mantra],
Empowering in the same manner that one has empowered the self,
One should worship [them] with the proper procedure. (v. 94)

Verse 94 (*svahṛdeti*). [First,] he should present to the assembled deities of the maṇḍala (*maṇḍalacakram*) oblations abounding in flowers, excellent sandalwood and so forth, consecrated by the muttered recitation (*-abhijaptaṃ*) of each seed-syllable (*svahṛdā-<svabījena-*). [Then] he should draw them towards the Pledge-maṇḍala, cause them to enter it, bind them to it and make them blissful in it by means of Yamāntaka[, Prajñāntaka, Padmāntaka and Vighnāntaka] respectively, and thereby (*-krameṇa*) cause them to permeate it as sesame oil permeates sandy soil. Then, with the proper procedure, namely, that which will be stated below, one should zealously (*prayataḥ*) worship (*abhyarccayet< pūjayet*) it, [that is to say, one should worship] the assembled deities (*-cakram*) of the maṇḍala, thus completed (*tad evaṃ {sa}pariniṣpanna[ṃ] maṇḍalacakra[ṃ]*), having [first] empowered them in the same manner that one has empowered the self (*svamiva*), [i.e.,] Mañjuvajra, through the sequence [of the four limbs] beginning with *sevā*. Here, the *sevā* is the process of generating (*niṣpattikramaḥ*) the maṇḍala-deities; the term common *sevā* is excessive *niṣyanda-phala*;

yat pūrvavac cakṣurādyadhiṣṭhānaṃ tat sāmānyopasodhanam adhimātra-vipākaphalam/ yat pūrvavac cittādyadhiṣṭhānaṃ{/} tat sāmānyasā[27b2]dhanam adhimātrapuruṣakāraphalam/ yaḥ pūrvavat jñānāṃbunābhiṣekakramas tat sāmānya[mahāsādhana]m adhimātravaimalyaphalaṃ/ abhiṣekānantarañ ca Vairocanāditathāgatānāṃ makuṭe A[27b3]kṣobhyo draṣṭavyaḥ/ evaṃ LocanāRūpavajrayoḥ Vairocanaḥ/ MāmakīŚabdavajrāDharmadhātuvajrāṇām Akṣobhyaḥ/ PāṇḍarāRasavajrādayor Amitābhaḥ[186]/ TārāSparśavajrayor[187] A[27b4] moghasiddhiḥ/ Gandhavajrā{vajrā}yā Ratnasambhavaḥ/ Yamāryādīnām uktā[188] evādhipata{v}ya iti//

pad naṅ raṅ gi sa bon 'di rnams kyis/
gzugs la sogs pa thams cad draṅs nas ni/
yaṅ dag byaṅ chub yid kyi ṅo bo yi[189]/
'od kyi dkyil 'khor dag tu bsgom par bya//95//

pad ma'i naṅ gi raṅ gi sa bon 'od kyis draṅs nas gzugs thams cad ni/ pad ma'i 'od zer dkyil 'khor yaṅ dag byaṅ chub yid kyi sa bon bsam par bya//95//

---

186. Ms.: Amitābhāḥ.

187. Ms.: Sparsavajrāyor.

188. Ms.: ukta.

189. Ms.: D. C.: yis.

the *upasādhana* is the empowerment of the eyes and other [sensual organs]; the *sādhana* is the empowerment of [the Three Vajras] beginning with Mind; and the *mahāsādhana* is the process of empowerment by the water of wisdom (*jñānāmbunā*). Each of these limbs is [now] common, and their results, respectively, *niṣyanda-*, *vipāka-*, *puruṣakāra-*, and *vaimalya-*, excessive; and each of the four process is as before [explained in verses 55–66]. Furthermore, immediately after the empowerment (*abhiṣeka-*) [of the deities] one should visualize Akṣobhya on the crowns of the [four] Buddhas beginning with Vairocana. Likewise, one should visualize Vairocana on [the crowns of] Locanā and Rūpavajrā; Akṣobhya on [the crowns of] Māmakī, Śabdavajrā and Dharmadhātuvajrā; Amitābha on [the crowns of] Pāṇḍarā and Rasavajrā; Amoghasiddhi on [the crowns of] Tārā and Sparśavajrā; and Ratnasambhava on [the crown of] Gandhavajrā. The lords of Yamāri and the other [gatekeepers] have already been stated.

With rays from one's seed[-syllables],
Drawing in Rūpa and all the other [deities],
One should meditate [on them] in the lotus
In the form of supreme Bodhicitta in a halo of light. (v. 95)

//tad evam āhitābhiṣekaṃ cakra[ṃ] yena vidhinā pūjayitavyaṃ/ tam vidhi[ṃ] **ka**[27b5]**malodara** (pad naṅ) ityādinā āryaṣaṭkena pūjāparyantenāha/ jñānasatvahṛdbījabhābhiḥ/ **sarvarūpādyām ākṛṣya** (gzugs la sogs pa thams cad draṅs nas ni) svaśarīre praveśya[190] vajramārganirgata[ṃ] kṛtvā **mayūkhamaṇḍala** ('od kyi dkyil 'khor) **bodhici**[27b6]**ttasvarūpaṃ** (byaṅ chub yid kyi ṅo bo yi) vidyā**kamalodare**[191] (pad naṅ) **dhyāyāt** (bsgom par bya)/

śes rab ba spu re re las byuṅ ba'i[192]/
'od zer rnam pa sna tshogs rgya chen tshogs/
ma lus nam mkha'i gtos ni kun tu khyab/
de la blo daṅ ldan pas rab tu spro//96//

śes rab so so'i ba spu las byuṅ sna tshogs rnam pa'i 'od zer rgyas pa'i tshogs/ ma lus khyab pa'i mkha' gźi thams cad de nas blo daṅ ldan pas spro bar bya//96//

190. Ms.: pravesya.

191. Ms.: kamalaudare.

192. P. N.: re las byuṅ ba yi.

[Now,] in the six *Āryā* [verses] that begin with the word "in the lotus" (*kamalodara*) and end with [the explanation of] the offerings, he explains the procedure by which one is to worship the assembly of deities after it has been consecrated in this way. [One] should draw in Rūpa (i.e., Vairocana) and all [the other deities] with rays from the seed[-syllable] of the Knowledge-being, make them enter one's body, emit them through the adamantine channel (*vajra-mārga* = penis), and meditate on them as [one's] Bodhicitta (i.e., semen) encircled by a halo of light (*mayūkhamaṇḍala-*) within the lotus (i.e., vagina) of the consort.

Then, a mass of rays of many colours
That pervades the whole sky,
Born from each pore of the consort—
One with wisdom should send them forth entirely. (v. 96)

ata iti tad evaṃ dhyātvā **prajñāprati**{rūpā}**romodbhavaṃ** (śes rab ba spu re re las byuṅ ba'i) **nānāvidharaśmi**[193]**vistaravyūhaṃ** ('od zer rnam pa sna tshogs rgya chen tshogs) **vyāptasarvākāśatalaṃ**[194] (nam mkha'i gtos ni kun tu khyab) {/} **matimān** (blo daṅ ldan pas) ity u[28a1]tsargādi[195]bhedabuddhirahitaḥ sann **abhitaḥ** (ma lus) sarvato bhāvena **protsṛjet** (rab tu spro)/

'od kyi sgo las ṅes par 'byuṅ ba yi/
yan lag dri med rgyan kun gyis legs brgyan/
me loṅ pi vaṅ dri daṅ ro yi snod/
gos daṅ chos 'byuṅ ba la sogs pa'i//97//

'od zer sgo nas 'byuṅ ba'i dri med thams cad rgyan gyis śin tu brgyan sku daṅ/ me loṅ pi vaṅ dri daṅ ro yi snod daṅ na bza' chos 'byuṅ la sogs daṅ//97//

tato **raśmi**[196]**mukhanirgatābhir** ('od kyi sgo las ṅes par 'byuṅ ba yi) **amalasarvābharaṇasvalaṅkṛtā**{bhi}**ṅgī** (yan lag dri med rgyan kun gyis legs brgyan)ti[197] rūpādidevatābhiḥ

193. Ms.: rasmi.

194. Ms: ākāsatalaṃ.

195. Ms.: iti utsargādi.

196. Ms.: rasmi.

197. Ms.: amalasarvābharaṇasvalaṅkṛtābhiṅgītī.

Verse 96 (*ata iti*). Then, that is to say, when one has accomplished this meditation, one should send forth (*protsṛjet*) entirely (*abhitaḥ<sarvato bhāvena*) from each pore of the consort['s body] an expanding mass of rays of many colours that pervades the whole sky, [doing so] with wisdom (*matimān*), [that is to say,] without clinging to the discriminative notion that there is a [real agent or a real object in this act of] emission.

The [goddesses] whose stainless bodies are beautifully adorned with various ornaments
Have come forth from the tips of the rays.
They have a mirror, a lute, a perfume [container], a food vessel,
A cloth, a *dharmodaya* and so forth, respectively. (v. 97)

Then [he should visualize that] the goddesses beginning with Rūpa[vajrā], whose stainless bodies are beautifully adorned with various ornaments, have come forth from the tips of the rays [that have been emitted from the pores of the consort].

mtshan mas rim gyis rnam par sgeg bcas śiṅ/
rol pa'i lag pa dam pa rnams daṅ ni/
'od kyi snaṅ bas sprul pa sna tshogs pa'i/
mchod pa'i sprin gyi dra bas khyab pa daṅ//98//

mtshan ma rnams kyi rim pas mdzes pas ldem bag phyag ni lo ma 'od daṅ bcas/
gsal ba'i 'od zer sprul pa maṅ po sna tshogs mchod pa'i sprin gyi dra ba rnams 'byuṅ daṅ//98//

krameṇe(rim gyis)ti yathākramaṃ [28a2]ṣaḍbhir darppaṇādi**cihnais** (mtshan mas) tadāyaiś[198] ca yathāyoga[ṃ] khaḍgapadmādibhir **vilasantī** (rnam par sgeg bcas śiṅ) śobhamānā[199] **salīlakara**[200]**pallavānām** (rol pa'i lag pa dam pa rnams daṅ ni) **ābhāvabhāsā**[201] ('od kyi snaṅ bas)/ yāsāñ ca bhāsvaṅgahastibhir **nirmitā** (sprul pa) **nānāpūjāṃbhujāla**[28a3]**visarā** (sna tshogs pa'i mchod pa'i sprin gyi dra bas khyab pa daṅ) rūpādipūjāmeghasamūhaprasārāḥ

198. Ms.: tathādyais.

199. Ms.: sobhamānā.

200. Ms.: salilakara.

201. Ms.: ābhāvāsā.

The splendour of their charming fingers is
Beautiful on account of the respective symbols,
And networks of cloud-like masses of offerings
Miraculously produced by [their] rays and splendour spread. (v. 98)

Verse 98 (*krameṇeti*). The splendour (*ābhāvabhāsa<yaśaḥ*) of their charming (*salīla-*) fingers (*karapallava-*) is [made all the more] beautiful (*vilasantī<śobhamānā*) by the respective symbols [in the principal hand] of each (*krameṇa<yathākramaṃ*), that is to say, the six principal hands of all of them], beginning with a mirror, and by the secondary (*tadādya-*) symbols as appropriate (*yathāyogam*) [in the other hands of all of them], that is to say, a sword, a lotus [and a wheel or jewel]. [He should] also [visualize] expanding cloud-like masses of the visible and other [classes of] offerings miraculouly produced by their radiant and lovely hands.

dṅos rnams sgyu ma la sogs so sor ni/
yaṅ dag rig ciṅ 'jig rten blta[202] mkhas pa/
rtog pa ma lus kun las ṅes grol źiṅ/
mchog tu bde ba bskyed pa'i rgyur gyur pa//99//

sgyu ma la sogs dra ba'i dṅos po so so yaṅ dag rig pa'i 'jig rten lta dge daṅ/
rtog pa thams cad ṅes grol mchog gi bde ba 'byuṅ rgyu'i dṅos ldan pa'i//99//

tābhir māyopamādi[203]rūpeṇa **vastūnāṃ** (dṅos rnams) yā **pratisamvit** (so sor ni yaṅ dag rig ciṅ)/ yā ca **lokadṛṣṭis** ('jig rten blta) tadviṣayānuraktāl lokānurūpanṛtagītādiparicayarūpāt[204][28a4] tayoḥ/ **kuśalābhi[r]**[205] (mkhas pas) **nirvikalpa** (rtog pa...ṅes grol źiṅ) **mahāsukhotpattihetubhūtābhiḥ** (mchog tu bde ba bskyed pa'i rgyur gyur pa)/

202. P. N.: lta.

203. Ms.: tābhiḥ māyopamādi.

204. Ms.: paricayarūpāta.

205. Ms.: kusalābhi.

With the skill in penetrating insight that things are illusory and so forth,
And [the skill] in the secular consciousness,
One should [turn] them into a means for causing the emergence of the great
bliss
Free of all conceptual notions. (v. 99)

[And he should meditate] on them as skilled both in the insight that [all] things are illusory and so forth[206] and in the secular consciousness that consists of serving [the deities] with dance, song and so forth conforming with [the desires of] the secular (*-loka-*), who are attached to these objects of the senses (*viṣayānurakta-*), and [finally] as causing the emergence of the great bliss that is free of [all] conceptual notions (*nirvikalpamahāsukha-*).

---

206. There are ten analogies for *śūnyatā*: 1. illusion (*māyā*), 2. mirage (*marīci*), water-moon (*udakacandra*), 4. space (*ākāśa*), 5. echo (*pratiśrutkā*), 6. imaginary city in the sky (*gandharvanagara*), 7. dream (*svapna*), 8. appearance (*pratibhāsa*), 9. mirror image (*pratibimba*), and 10. magic (*nirmita*).

gzugs la sogs pa'i lha mo rnams daṅ ni/
de bźin phyi yi dri sogs thams cad kyis/
rgyal ba'i dbaṅ po rnams ni legs mchod ciṅ/
de ltar tha dad rtogs las[207] ṅes grol bya//100//

gzugs la sogs pa'i lha mo rnams kyis de bźin phyi ma'i dri sogs thams cad kyis/ dbye ba'i rtog pa grol bas rgyal ba'i dbaṅ po rnams la yaṅ dag mchod par bya//100//

Oṃ sarvatathāgatapūjāvajrasvabhāvātmako 'haṃ/

tad evaṃbhūtā**Rūpavajrādidevībhis** (gzugs la sogs pa'i lha mo rnams) **tadvad** (de bźin) **bāhyaiś**[208] (phyi yi) ca **sa[r]vagandhādyai[r]** (dri sogs thams cad kyis) **jinendrān**[209] (rgyal ba'i dbaṅ po rnams ni) maṇḍalacakrāntargatān/ Oṃ sarvatathā[28a5]gata[pūjā]vajrasvabhāvātmako 'haṃ/ ity **evaṃ** (de ltar) pūjādhiṣṭhānamantreṇa pūjyapūjakapūjā**bhedavikalpanirmukta**(dad rtog las ṅes grol)yogī **saṃpūjayed** (legs mchod ciṅ) iti//

---

207. P. N.: rtog la.

208. Ms.: bahyais.

209. Ms.: jinendrāna.

Making offerings to the Kings of Victors
Through Rūpa[vajrā] and other goddesses,
As well as external offerings such as incense,
In this way, one should deliver free of dualistic awareness. (v. 100)

Oṃ sarvatathāgatapūjāvajrasvabhāvātmako 'haṃ/

[Then,] just as the yogi [has made these mental offerings] through Rūpavajrā and the other goddesses as above (*evaṃbhūta-*), so he should worship the Buddhas in the assembly of the maṇḍala with external offerings such as the various fragrant substances, in this way (*evaṃ*), namely, using the mantra that empowers the offerings: "*Oṃ sarvatathāgata[pūjā]vajra svabhāvātmako 'ham,*" [Oṃ, I embody the adamantine nature of (offering of) all the Buddhas], [while remaining] free of the dualistic awareness (*-vikalpa-*) that differentiates the offerer, the recipient and the act of offering.

sgra yi yul rnams ma lus pa rnams ni/
brag ca'i sgra 'drar ṅes brtags de[210] rjes la/
raṅ[211] yid lhag pa'i lha ru gnas pa la/
chos rnams bstod pa'i sgra ni byed par bsam//101//

de yi 'og tu sgra brñan 'dra bar sgra yul thams cad la ni yod bsams na/ raṅ yid rig pa'i lha yi bstod pa'i sgra daṅ ldan pa'i chos rnams źes su gsuṅs//101//

//idānīṃ stotropahāram āha/ pratiśabdety[212]ādi/ **ta**[28a6]**danv** (de rjes la) iti pūjāvidher[213] anantaraṃ **pratiśabdavat** (brag ca'i sgra 'drar) samastastutirūpa-śabdagrāman[214] **nirūpayan** (ṅes brtag)/ **svamanasy** (raṅ yid) ev**ādhidevatāṃ**[215] (lhag pa'i lha ru) pradhānadevatā[ṃ]/ tasya **stutyā** (stod pa'i) sukha san **dharmān** (chos rnams) pratibhāsārū[28b1][pa]

---

210. P. N.: der.

211. P. N.: yaṅ.

212. Ms.: pratisabdety.

213. Ms.: pūjāvidhir.

214. Ms.: sabdagrāma.

215. Ms.: adhidevataṃ.

After that, considering the totality of sounds thoroughly
As [unsubstantial] like an echo,
[Next,] contemplating the main deity in one's heart,
One [should] metamorphose them into a eulogium of Dharmas. (v. 101)

Now, in the verse beginning with the word "Echo" (*pratiśabda*), he explains the offering that is in the form of a hymn of praise. Thereafter (*tadanu*), that is to say, immediately after the presentation of the offerings, he should contemplate the main deity (*adhidevatāṃ<pradhānadevatāṃ*) in his heart while perceiving the collection of sounds that constitutes the eulogium as an echo....

akṣobhyavajra mahājñāna vajradhātu mahābudha/
trimaṇḍala trivajrāgra ghoṣa vajra namo 'stu te//102//
(= *Guhyasamāja* XVII,1)

[....a]**kṣobhyaḥ**/ sa evābhedyatvād **vajraḥ** suviśuddha[216][dharmadhātu-jñānātmakatvāt] **mahājñānaḥ**/ abhedyaḥ/.....[28b2][?]dhatvād **vajradhātu mahābudhaḥ**[217]/ kāyavākcittamaṇḍalātmakatvāt **trimaṇḍalaḥ**/ kāyādivajreṣu cittasya pradhānatvāt **trivajrāgraḥ**/ evaṃbhūtam Akṣobhyañ ca pratipadaṃ saṃbodhya **namo [']stu te**[28b3]ti namas tubhya[ṃ] stutimukhebhyo dharmā[n] āhuḥ[218]/ **ghoṣe**ty pradeśaya/ **vajre**ty advaitadharmatām ity arthaḥ/

vairocana mahāśuddha vajraśānta mahārata/
prakṛtiprabhāsvarān dharmān[219] deśa vajra namo 'stu te//103//
(= *Guhyasamāja* XVII,2)

---

216. Ms.: suvisuddha.

217. Ms.: mahābuddha.

218. Ms.: āhaḥ.

219. Tibetan translation of *Samantabhadra* and Sanskrit verse from the *Guhyasamāja* do not tally in pāda C. Ms. tallies with Tibetan translation of *Samantabhadra: raṅ bźin 'od gsal mchog gi mchog.*

O Akṣobhyavajra, great wisdom,
Great sage of the diamond-realm,
Triple maṇḍala, the chief of the triple adamant,
Adamantine one! Proclaim aloud! Homage to you! (v. 102)

He is Akṣobhya and is also the adamantine one (*vajra*) because he is indestructible. He is great wisdom (*mahājñāna*) because he has the wisdom of the pure dharma-realm.... He is the diamond-realm (*vajradhātu*) because.... He is the triple maṇḍala (*trimaṇḍala*) because he has the nature of body and so forth (i.e., body, speech and mind). He is the chief of the triple adamant (*trivajrāgra*) because the adamantine mind is the most important in the triple adamant. In this way, praising such Akṣobhya in each quarter, he explains the dharma by means of a paean paying homage to you (*namo 'stu te<namas tubhyam*). "Proclaim aloud" (*ghoṣa*) is imperative. The adamantine one (*vajra*) means the non-dual nature of the dharma.

O Vairocana, great purity,
Adamantine peace, great joy,
Dharma of the clear light,
Adamantine one! Please explain! Homage to you! (v. 103)

evam virocanād **Vairocanaḥ**/ niḥkleśasatvān **mahāśuddha**[220] abhedyaśāntika[221]ka [28b4]rmmādhipatyād **vajraśāntaḥ**[222]/ paramānandātmakatvān **mahārata** ādarśajñānātmakatvāt **prakṛtiprabhāsvarāṇām agra**/ evam saṃbodhya **deśa vajra namo [']stu ta** iti pūrvavad āhu[ḥ]/

ratnarāja sugāmbhīrya khavajrākāśanirmala/
svabhāvaśuddha nirlepa kāyavajra namo 'stu te//104//
(= *Guhyasamāja* XVII,3)

ratnarāje[28b5]ti ratnasambhavaḥ/ suṣṭhugāmbhīryatvāt **sugāmbhīrya**/ ākāśavad [223]abhedyavajratvāt **khavajraḥ**/ samatājñānatvād **ākāśanirmmalaḥ**[224] sa{ta} eva **svabhāvaśuddha**[225]kleśakarmajanmajñeyavāsanā[28b6]malavigamān **nirlepa** ...ākāśavat...[kāyavajra] **namo [']stu ta** iti pūrvavad āhu[ḥ]/

---

220. Ms.: mahāsuddha.

221. Ms.: sāntika.

222. Ms.: vajrasāntaḥ.

223. Ms.: ākāsavad.

224. Ms.: ākāsanirmmalaḥ.

225. Ms.: suddha.

He is Vairocana (i.e., shining one) because he is radiant. He is great purity (*mahāśuddha*) because he is lacking affliction (*kleśa*). He is adamantine peace (*vajraśānta*) because he is the chief of indestructible performance of propitiation (*śāntikakarma*). He is great joy (*mahārata*) because he has the nature of supreme joy (*paramānanda*). He is the foremost of the clear light (*prakṛti-prabhāsvarāṇām agra*) because he has the nature of the mirror-like wisdom. Speaking in this way, "O adamantine one! Please explain!" (*deśa vajra namo* [']*stu te*) and so forth is the same as above.

O king of jewels, extreme deepness,
Adamantine space, space-like purity,
Pure in nature, stainless!
Homage to the adamantine body! (v. 104)

The king of jewels (*ratnarāja*) is Ratnasambhava. He is deepness (*sugāmbhīrya*) because he is exceedingly profound. He is adamantine space (*khavajraḥ*) because he is indestructible like space. He is space-like purity (*ākāśanirmmalaḥ*) because he has the wisdom of equality. And he is also stainless (*nirlepa*) because he is pure in his nature and destroys rebirth caused by afflictions.... "Homage to the adamantine body!" (*kāyavajra namo* [']*stu te*) and so forth is the same as above.

vajrāmṛta mahārāja nirvikalpa khavajradhṛk/
rāgapāramitāprāpta bhāṣavajra namo 'stu te//105//
(= *Guhyasamāja* XVII,4)

vajrāmṛtety amitābha....

O adamantine immortal one, great king,
Free from conceptual notions, holder of adamantine space,
Who has achieved the transcendence of passion!
Homage to adamantine speech! (v. 105)

The adamantine immortal (*vajrāmṛta*) is Amitābha....

ビブリオグラフィー (Bibliography)

【邦文】[Japanese]

加納和雄[Kano, Kazuo] 2014, 「普賢成就法の新出梵文資料について」[Newly Available Sanskrit Material of Jñānapāda's *Samantabhadrasādhana*]『密教学研究』第46号。

菊谷竜太[Ryuta, Kikuya] 2003, 「ジュニャーナパーダ流の修習次第」[Jñānapāda's *Dvikramatattvabhāvanā-Mukhāgama*]『印度学仏教学研究』51-2。

佐藤努[Sato, Tsutomu] 1995, 「ジニャーナパーダ流のマンダラ構成」[The Composition of Maṇḍala in the Jñānapāda-school]『密教図像』第14号。

田中公明[Tanaka, Kimiaki] 1996, 『インド・チベット曼荼羅の研究』[Studies in the Indo-Tibetan maṇḍala](法藏館)。

— 2010, 『インドにおける曼荼羅の成立と発展』[Genesis and Development of the Maṇḍala in India] (春秋社)。

田中公明[Tanaka, Kimiaki]・吉崎一美[Yoshizaki, Kazumi]1998, 『ネパール仏教』[Nepalese Buddhism](春秋社)。

松長有慶[Matsunaga, Yukei] 1978, 『秘密集会タントラ校訂梵本』[The Guhyasamāja tantra](東方出版)。

— 1980, 『密教経典成立史論』[A history of the formation of esoteric Buddhist scriptures](法藏館)。

【欧文】[Western Languages]

Apple, James B. 2016. "The Knot Tied with Space": Notes on a Previously Unidentified Stanza in Buddhist Literature and Its Citation, *The Indian International Journal of Buddhist Studies* 17.

Bahulkar, S. S. 2010. *Śrīguhyasamājamaṇḍalavidhiḥ*. Sarnath: CIHTS.

Bandurski, Frank 1994, "Übersicht über die Göttinger Sammlungen der von Rāhula Sāṅkṛtyāyana in Tibet aufgefundenen buddhistischen Sanskrit-Texte (Funde buddhistischer Sanskrit-Handschriften, III)," in Bechert Heinz (ed.), Sanskrit-Wörterbuch der buddhistischen Texte aus den Turfan-Funden, Beiheft 5, Göttingen: Vandenhoeck & Ruprecht.

Chakravarti, Chintaharan. 1984. *Guhyasamājatantrapradīpodyotanaṭīkā*. Patna: K. P. Jayaswal Research Institute.

Sāṅkṛi(sic)tyāyana, Rāhula 1937. "Second Search of Sanskrit Palm-leaf Mss. in Tibet," J.B.O.R.S., Vol.XXIII, Part I, Patna: The Bihar and Orissa Research Society.

Sferra, Francesco. 2008. "Sanskrit Manuscripts and Photographs of Sanskrit Manuscripts in Giuseppe Tucci's Collection," in Francesco Sferra (ed.), *Sanskrit Texts from Giuseppe Tucci's Collection*, Part I. Roma: Is.I.A.O..

Vaidya, P. L., ed. 1960. *Madhyamakaśāstra of Nāgārjuna with the Commentary: Prasannapadā by Candrakīrti*. Darbhanga: Mithila Institute.

Wayman, Alex. 1977. *Yoga of the Guhyasamājatantra*. Delhi: Motilal Banarsidass.

【藏文】[Tibetan]

Deb ther sṅon po, Vol.1, 成都 1984, pp.446-452.

【中文】[Chinese]

中国藏学研究中心(CTRC) 1998,『丹珠爾』(対勘本) 第21巻, 北京: 中国藏学出版社。

Samantabhadra nāma Sādhana

【ネパール語】[Nepalese]

Pūrṇaratna Vajrācārya 1967, *Bṛhatsūcīpatram*, Bauddhaviṣayaka Vol.1, Kathmandu: Vīrapustakālaya, Vikrama saṃvat 2023 (≒1967).

Hemarāja Śākya 1974, *Nepāla Lipi-Prakāśa*, Kathmandu: Nepāla rājakīya prajñā pratiṣṭhāna, Vikrama saṃvat 2030 (≒ 1974).

あとがき

本書は、これまで著者が、1990年から2010年まで、複数の学術書・学術誌に発表してきた『普賢成就法』サンスクリット註の研究をまとめた、日英二カ国語版の研究書である。(p.153「初出一覧」参照)

『秘密集会タントラ』には「聖者流」「ジュニャーナパーダ流」という二大流派があるが、「聖者流」に比して、「ジュニャーナパーダ流」の研究は立ち遅れている。その原因の一つは、「聖者流」の重要典籍のサンスクリット原典がネパールで発見され、校訂テキストが出版されているのに対し、ネパールからは、「ジュニャーナパーダ流」のサンスクリット原典が発見されていなかったからである。ところが著者が、ニューヨークのIASWRが頒布したネパールのサンスクリット写本*Mañjuvajramukhyākhyāna*を分析したところ、『秘密集会』「ジュニャーナパーダ流」を特徴づける文殊金剛十九尊曼荼羅の儀軌であることが判明した。ただしこのテキストは、インド撰述の儀軌に基づき、ネパールで編集されたものと思われた。しかしネパールに「ジュニャーナパーダ流」の儀軌が存在することから、それが参照したであろうインド撰述の「ジュニャーナパーダ流」のテキストも残存している可能性が高まった。そこで1988年から1989年にかけてNepal Research Centreの客員研究員としてネパールに留学したのを機に、『秘密集会』系の密教写本を捜索したところ、この『普賢成就法』サンスクリット註を発見したのである。

しかし著者は、本写本のような註釈文献に慣れていなかったため、解読は難航した。ところが1993年にOxford大学Spalding財団客員研究員として英国短期留学した折、アレクシス・サンダーソン教授の懇切な指導を受け、本文献の英訳を完成させることができた。そこで著者の博士論文である『インドにおける曼荼羅の成立と発展』（春秋社、2010年）の第２部には、これまでに発表してきたローマ字化テキストの改訂版と、その和訳を収録した。しかし文献概説とテキストの英訳については、いままで発表の機会を得なかった。

そこで2015年に日本学術振興会より科研費の受給が決定したのを機に、以前に発表したローマ字化テキストと英訳を対照させ、さらに文献概説とビブリオグラフィーを付して、一冊のモノグラフとして刊行することにした。

文献概説で紹介したように、『普賢成就法』や、その註釈類のサンスクリット写本が、チベット自治区に所蔵されていることが明らかになったが、外国の研究者には公開されていない。中国国内のサンスクリット写本が外国で公開される場合、中国の研究者と欧米の大学・研究機関の共同プロジェクトとなることが多い。小さな民間の研究機関に属する著者が、このようなプロジェクトに参画する可能性は、ほとんどないといってよい。日本の研究者が、どのようなパイオニア的な研究をし、どれだけの事実を明らかにしたのかを英語で発表しておかないと、将来、外国において当該分野の研究が進捗しても、これまでの日本の研究が、完全に無視されることになりかねない。著者が、本書のような、日英二カ国語のインド・チベット仏教のモノグラフ刊行に力を入れているのは、そのためである。

本書の刊行が、密教やチベット仏教に関心をもつ海外の研究者に、一定の新情報を提供するものになることは疑いない。それが機縁となり、日本と海外の学術交流が盛んになることを期待している。本書を、大学や留学先で指導を受けた先生方、かつての同僚、そして海外の友人に贈ることを楽しみにしている。

本書の刊行に当たっては、多くの方々のお世話になった。とくにアレクシス・サンダーソン教授には、オックスフォード大学留学中に本写本研究のご指導を頂いた。また畏友ロルフ・ギーブル氏には、英文校閲だけでなく、種々の有益な助言を頂戴した。チベット大学（サールナート）のチャンバ・サムテン教授には、著者が書いた拙いチベット語要旨を校閲して頂いた。ネパール国立公文書館のサウバーギヤ・プラダーナーンガ館長からは写本の撮影許可を頂戴し、藤田アーカイブスからは文殊金剛曼荼羅の写真の掲載許可を頂いた。また英文校閲費と非売品180部（献本用）の印刷費は、日本学術振興会の科研費基盤研究（C）「インド・チベット密教と曼荼羅の研究」（課題番号: 15K02050）から支弁した。さらに本書の刊行を引き受けられた（有）渡辺出版の渡辺潔社長にも大変お世話になった。末筆となって恐縮であるが、記して感謝の意を表したい。

2016年11月26日

著者

Postscript

This volume is a Japanese-English bilingual study of the Sanskrit commentary on the *Samantabhadra nāma sādhana* which I had previously published in instalments on different occasions between 1990 and 2010.

There are two main lineages deriving from the *Guhyasamāja-tantra*—the Ārya school and the Jñānapāda school. In the study of the *Guhyasamāja-tantra*, research into the Jñānapāda school has lagged behind that of the Ārya school, and the chief reason for this has been the fact that, in contrast to the Ārya school, none of the Sanskrit originals of any of its basic texts had been discovered in Nepal.

About thirty yeas ago, I discovered that a manuscript entitled *Mañjuvajramukhyākhyāna*, included among the Buddhist Sanskrit manuscripts in the microfiche collection of the Institute for Advanced Studies of World Religions (IASWR) in New York, is a ritual manual of the nineteen-deity maṇḍala of Mañjuvajra characteristic of the Jñānapāda school. Unfortunately, the *Mañjuvajramukhyākhyāna* appears to have been compiled in Nepal on the basis of a ritual manual of the Jñānapāda school of Indian provenance, but the existence of such a manual suggested that there was a strong possibility that the original Sanskrit manuscript of Indian origin on which it was based had also been preserved in Nepal.

Subsequently I was able to visit Nepal in 1988-89 as a visiting research fellow at the Nepal Research Centre, and taking advantage of this opportunity, I eagerly searched through Sanskrit manuscripts associated with the Guhyasamāja cycle. Eventually I discovered a Sanskrit commentary on the *Samantabhadra nāma sādhana*, but the study of the manuscript proved difficult since I was not accustomed to reading such commentaries in Sanskrit.

During a period of study at Oxford as a Spalding visiting fellow in 1993, I was able to complete an English translation of the text under the kind guidance of Prof. Alexis Sanderson. I then included a revised edition of the romanized text, which I had previously published in Japan, and a Japanese translation in Part II of my dissertation, *Genesis and Development of the Maṇḍala in India* (Tokyo: Shunjūsha, 2010). But at the time I had no opportunity to publish my introduction and translation of the text in English.

Later, having received financial support from the Japan Society for the Promotion of Science in 2015, I started to revise my previously published articles with a view to bringing them together as a monograph with an introduction in English and a bibliography.

As was noted in the introduction to this volume, recent studies have made it clear that Sanskrit manuscripts of the *Samantabhadra* and its commentary are preserved in the Tibet Autonomous Region. However, they are not accessible to foreign researchers. In many cases, Sanskrit manuscripts preserved in China are published through joint research projects between Chinese scholars and Euro-American universities or research institutes. It is very difficult for a researcher like myself, belonging to a small private research institute, to participate in such joint projects between China and other countries. But if Japanese scholars do not publish their research and academic findings in English, their research may end up being completely overlooked even when their findings may help to advance research overseas. This is why I have made the effort to publish Japanese-English bilingual monographs dealing with

Indo-Tibetan Buddhist studies.

This volume should provide some new information to foreign readers interested in esoteric Buddhism and Tibetan Buddhism and will, I hope, contribute to academic exchange between Japan and other countries. I look forward to presenting copies to teachers, former colleagues, and friends abroad.

Lastly, I would like to offer my heartful thanks to all those who have helped in the preparation of this publication, including Prof. Alexis Sanderson, who supervised my study at Oxford; Mr. Rolf Giebel, who oversaw the English translation and gave me helpful advice; Prof. Jampa Samten, who oversaw the Tibetan summary; Ms. Saubhāgya Pradhānāṅga, the chief of the National Archives, Nepal, who provided me with the photograph of the manuscript; the Fujita Archives, which provided me with the photograph of the Mañjuvajra-maṇḍala; the Japan Society for the Promotion of Science, which provided financial support (JPS KAKENHI Grant number: 15K02050) for the translation and for the printing costs for 180 non-commercial copies from fiscal 2015 to fiscal 2017; and Mr. Kiyoshi Watanabe, the president of Watanabe Publishing Co., Ltd., who undertook to publish this book with great care.

26 November 2016

Kimiaki TANAKA

『普賢成就法』関係論文の初出一覧

章節	写本	掲載誌	発表年	論文タイトル
		『東方』第6号	平成2年（1990年）	ネパールのサンスクリット語仏教文献研究(2)—NGMPPで新たに撮影された密教写本を中心として—
(1)	21a1-23a6	『＜我＞の思想(前田専学博士還暦記念論文集)』(春秋社)	平成3年（1991年）	『秘密集会』ジュニャーナパーダ流の生起次第caturaṅgaの新資料 －National Archives pra. 1697(kha 2)の研究－
(2)	23b1-27a4	『密教図像』16号	平成9年（1997年）	新出のSkt. 写本『普賢成就法註』所説の文殊金剛十九尊曼荼羅について
(3)	27a4-28b6	『東洋文化研究所紀要』150冊	平成19年（2007年）	Buddhajñānapādaの *Samantabhadra nāma sādhana* における曼荼羅の供養次第
		『インドにおける曼荼羅の成立と発展』(春秋社)	平成22年（2010年）	ジュニャーナパーダの『普賢成就法』註概説
				『普賢成就法』Skt. 註—テキストと和訳—

著者略歴

田中公明(たなかきみあき)

1955(昭和30)年、福岡県八幡市(現北九州市)生まれ。東京大学文学部卒(印度哲学専攻)、1984年同大学大学院博士課程満期退学。同大学文学部助手(文化交流)を経て、1988年(財)東方研究会[現(公財)中村元東方研究所]専任研究員。2008年、東京大学大学院より博士[文学]号を取得。2013年、学位論文『インドにおける曼荼羅の成立と発展』(春秋社)で鈴木学術財団特別賞を受賞。

東京大学(1992, 1994～1996, 2001～2004年)、拓殖大学(1994, 1998年)、大正大学綜合佛教研究所(2016年)、高野山大学(2016年)等で非常勤講師、北京日本学研究センター短期派遣教授(2003, 2010年)を歴任。現在(2017年)、富山県南砺市利賀村「瞑想の郷」主任学芸員、チベット文化研究会副会長。東方学院(2001年～)、慶應義塾大学(2001年～)、東洋大学大学院(2017)講師[いずれも非常勤]、ネパール留学(1988～89年)、英国オックスフォード大学留学(1993年)。韓国ハンビッツ文化財団学術顧問(1997～2015年)として、同財団の公式図録『チベット仏教絵画集成』第1巻～第7巻(臨川書店)を編集。密教、仏教図像、チベット学に関する著訳書(共著を含む)50冊、論文約150点。

詳しくは個人HP

http://www.geocities.jp/dkyil_hkhor/

を参照。

About the Author

Dr Kimiaki TANAKA (b.1955, Fukuoka) studied Indian Philosophy and Sanskrit Philology at the University of Tokyo. He received a doctorate in literature from the University of Tokyo in 2008 for his dissertation entitled "Genesis and Development of the Maṇḍala in India." It was published in 2010 by Shunjūsha with financial support from the Japan Society for the Promotion of Science and was awarded the Suzuki Research Foundation Special Prize in 2013.

He has been lecturer at the University of Tokyo, at Takushoku University, at the Institute for Comprehensive Studies of Buddhism, Taisho University (Genesis and Development of the Mandala) and at Koyasan University (Genesis and Development of the Mandala), teaching Tibetan as well as courses on Buddhism. He studied abroad as a visiting research fellow (1988-89) at Nepal Research Centre (Kathmandu) and held a Spalding Visiting Fellowship at Oxford University (Wolfson College) in 1993. As a visiting professor, he gave lectures on Sino-Japanese cultural exchange at Beijing Centre for Japanese Studies in 2003 and 2010.

From 1997 to 2015, he was the academic consultant to the Hahn Cultural Foundation (Seoul) and completed 7 vol. catalogue of their collection of Tibetan art entitled *Art of Thangka*. He is presently (2017) lecturer at Tōhō Gakuin, in Art History at Keio University (Buddhist Iconography) and in graduate course at Toyo University (Esoteric Buddhism). He is also chief curator of the Toga Meditation Museum in Toyama prefecture, the Vice-President of the Tibet Culture Centre International in Tokyo. He has published more than 50 books and 150 articles on Esoteric Buddhism, Buddhist Iconography and Tibetan art. http://www.geocities.jp/dkyil_hkhor/

梵文『普賢成就法註』研究

平成29年7月28日　第一刷発行

著　者　田中公明

発行者　渡辺 潔

発行所　有限会社渡辺出版
〒113-0033
東京都文京区本郷5丁目18番19号
電話　03-3813-2330
振替　00150-8-15495

印刷所　シナノ書籍印刷株式会社

ISBN978-4-902119-27-5

Samantabhadra nāma sādhana-ṭīkā

— Romanized Sanskrit Text and English Translation —

Date of Publication: 28 July 2017

Author: Kimiaki Tanaka

Publisher: Watanabe Publishing Co., Ltd.
5-18-19 Hongo, Bunkyo-ku
Tokyo 113-0033 Japan
tel/fax: 03-3813-2330
e-mail: watanabe.com@bloom.ocn.ne.jp

Printer: SHINANO BOOK PRINTING Co., Ltd.

Distributor (Outside of Japan): Biblia Impex Pvt. Ltd.
2/18, Ansari Road, New Delhi-110002, India
tel: +91-11-2327 8034　fax: +91-11-2328 2047
e-mail: contact@bibliaimpex.com

©Kimiaki TANAKA 2017 Printed in Japan
ISBN978-4-902119-27-5